TRADITIONAL COUNTRY CRAFTS

ALISON JENKINS

TRADITIONAL COUNTRY CRAFTS

ALISON JENKINS

WITH AN INTRODUCTION
BY TESSA EVELEGH

CASSELL

First published 1994
by Cassell
Villiers House
41/47 Strand
London WC2N 5JE

British Library Cataloguing-in-Publication Data
A catalogue record for this book is available from the British Library

ISBN 0-304-34438-9

This book was designed and produced by
Quintet Publishing Limited
6 Blundell Street
London N7 9BH

Creative Director: Richard Dewing
Designer: Isobel Gillan
Senior Editor: Laura Sandelson
Photographer: Paul Forrester

With thanks to Appalachia, the Folk Art Shop, for lending materials for
photography and to Mavis Jenkins for working the sampler.

Typeset in Great Britain by
Central Southern Typesetters, Eastbourne
Manufactured in Singapore by Bright Arts Pte. Ltd.
Printed in Singapore by Star Standard Pte. Ltd.

CONTENTS

THE CREATIVE CHARM
OF COUNTRY CRAFTS

NOTHING CAN BE more absorbing than the creative process. First, there is the vision of producing something beautiful and unique from what seems to be an unlikely pile of raw materials. Then as a form gradually begins to take shape, the mind can be emptied of all but minutiae, such as what colour to choose next, or how long it will take to do the next section, in what amounts to a creative form of relaxation.

The key to trying out the traditional crafts ourselves does not mean looking back, shunning new ideas. Folk art never did stand still. It gradually metamorphosed over the years as each maker added a little of his or her personality into each successive piece. Today, we can benefit from a rich visual encyclopaedia of shapes, colours and forms, and tested methods of working, while continuing to develop the craft, just as folk artists did in the past.

The danger we face nowadays when working on craft projects is the inclination to try to emulate the perfect finishes of factory-made products. This is a mistake. It is much better to forget the impersonal cloning of mass production, and to understand that the aim of "perfection" is not only misplaced, but can stop us from even starting a project for fear that our work will not be "good" enough.

*The Amish religion forbade intricate patchwork, lest it led to pride.
The resulting simple patchworks in surprisingly vibrant colours
demonstrate the truth of "less is more".*

In pre-industrial revolution days everything had to be handmade. Perhaps folk then were less exacting judges of their handiwork, keeping the faultless for best, and letting the slightly less beautiful fulfil the workaday needs. We also need

*This two-dimensional wooden chicken is inspired by the less
common, though nonetheless authentic traditional two-dimensional
decoys. This one was made by Sally Lazar from North Carolina.*

Garlands are traditional country decorations, and could be made from almost anything. This arrangement, fashioned from gingerbread men, cranberries and bay leaves, comes from Kentucky.

to remember that, because communities had to make everything for themselves, they were doubtless more accomplished craftspeople. They learned their skills from an early age – girls had usually stitched their first rudimentary sampler by the time they were five – and by that age, Shetland Islanders in Scotland already knew purl from plain. Little wonder that Shetland hand-knits still have the reputation for being among the best in the world.

Nowadays, we expect instant excellence from ourselves. Disappointment at an early stage can mean we lay the tools of a craft aside for life after only one attempt. That is a shame, because very often the reason we feel we have "failed" is that we have tried to tackle too ambitious a first project. Simplicity has never lacked beauty. The Amish people of the USA demonstrated the magnificence of uncomplicated patchwork made with just a few pieces by juxtaposing plain colours that either quietly complemented each other, or sang out vibrantly to-

gether. A successful first attempt offers great encouragement. Perfecting skills to produce ever more elaborate pieces is part of the enjoyment of craft work.

In centuries past, whenever people made things, they put a little of themselves into their work, improving their skills and developing their art form as they did so. The appeal is the unselfconscious way in which folk artists worked. Professional artists, who had studied, and were conscious of contemporary artistic movements, produced fine pieces but their work sometimes lost its innocence along the way.

Folk art was open to everyone. Rich in imagery, it lent insight into peoples and their histories as it developed and matured. The visual arts were even more relevant in the centuries before the printed word was available to all than they are today. Messages had to be conveyed in motifs, many of which held a symbolism etched deep into the consciousness of the people. This, in its turn, led to a rich visual vocabulary - ready tools for folk design. Symbolic sun, moon and stars, rooted in pagan times, are common to many cultures the world over. Layered on these are the icons of the different religions, which travelled with peoples as they migrated across continents and oceans.

These delightful elephant dolls are dressed in traditional Shaker-style homespun fabric.

The folk art of North America from the 18th century holds particular fascination because it became a melting pot of cultures. Many groups came to America seeking religious freedom and for that reason, kept themselves isolated. So influences rooted in one mother country became freed in another to develop in entirely different directions. A dramatic example of this is the contrast between the plain but brightly coloured quilts produced by the Amish people, and the more flamboyant appliqué quilts worked by the Lutherans. Both were sects of reformed Christians from southern Germany and Switzerland. Other examples show a cross-filtration of ideas. Crafts borrowed from American Indians were refined and adapted by settlers. Shaker baskets and decoy ducks both have roots in Indian traditions.

Without the benefits of a developed infrastructure comparable to those they left behind in Europe, settlers had to fall back on their own resources. There were not enough people for any but the most fundamental divisions of labour, so folk would "have a go" at whatever they could. Ministers and schoolmasters would carefully script certificates; blacksmiths tried fashioning weathervanes; farmers carved decoy ducks; and tavern sign-painters branched out into portrait- or landscape-painting. Sometimes lacking the technical skills to emulate academic artists, these folk artists found easier ways to create the look they wanted. Motifs were simplified, outline shapes were cut from stencils, and moulds were made to create form. Paintings were done to formulae and illustrations used the strokes learned in calligraphy.

These are all tricks we can borrow from the past. So, if we lack the dexterity of an accomplished draughtsman, or an artist's natural gift of composition, we could cut a selection of stencils from motifs found in magazines, and try out compositions before pencil ever needs to touch paper. That way, we could dispense with the worry of creating our own well-proportioned outlines or clever arrangements, while taking the opportunity to work on colour, shading and detail, if we want.

Amish rag dolls were rarely given features, as this was considered to make them too similar to pagan idols. These dolls were made by Cindi Hurlbut of Illinois.

Festive decorations were made from everyday materials threaded on to string or raffia. Here, bay leaves and cinnamon sticks join forces with corn on the cob and cranberries.

Colour choices, in almost any medium, are probably the greatest deciding factor in the success of a project. This goes a long way toward the appeal of folk craft. Until the 20th century, most pigments used for paints, stains and dyes came from natural sources, such as plants, flowers and clays, creating sympathetic colours. Modern synthetic colours tend to be brasher, but colouring has become so sophisticated that endless subtle variations are now available. The trick is to draw inspiration from the shades of yesteryear, aiming for as close a match as possible using modern materials which are often easier to handle.

The use of paints and other modern materials and equipment are perfectly legitimate in the tradition of folk art. Previous generations used whatever was available to them, so there is no reason why we should not use modern innovations

to make life easier. If you can enlarge a motif to exactly the right size on the photocopier, why not do so? Or if iron-on bonding web holds an appliqué motif in place while you stitch, so much the better. This is the stuff of developing folk art. It is not about copying exactly something that was done in the past – it is about drawing inspiration and adding our own touches.

This is the very spirit of this book. Insight into why and how particular crafts developed gives a deeper understanding of both the methods and the philosophies behind them.

The individually designed projects in the book, complete with instructions, are tasters to get you started. Each one is a testimony to the truth that handmade can be beautiful without being complicated. Enjoy gathering the materials you need for the project, and adding style with colour choices to suit your home – and making adaptations that offer space for your own creative expression.

MAKING THE USEFUL BEAUTIFUL

Artists – both fine and folk – have always dedicated themselves to the decorative, perfecting their skills and developing their creative expression on artefacts to be displayed and enjoyed as pieces of art. But what of everyday possessions? The utilitarian? The mundane?

Shaker Excellence

Day-to-day life becomes so much richer when we are surrounded by beautiful things. The most ordinary workaday items can be pleasing if they are well proportioned. The quest for efficiency often produces those elegant lines. The well-balanced basket that is easy to carry, the tool that has been perfectly weighted to make using it all the easier, have a natural harmony that is easy on the eye.

However the discipline of discarding embellishment makes more demands on design and materials. There are no patterns or trims to disguise incongruous dimensions or rough components.

It was this quality in design that the Shaker community understood more than 100 years ago. "Don't make anything if it is not useful," their philosophy goes, "but if it is both useful and necessary, don't hesitate to make it beautiful as long as the decorative elements are an inherent part of the design and don't interfere with function." This wisdom, along with the particular and puritan Shaker lifestyle, led to the design and making of exquisitely proportioned furniture and household items that were held up as paragons of quality in their time and are much sought after today.

The Shakers' mixed but celibate communal living meant that there were plenty of hands to deal with the chores and distracting minutiae of life, such as the paying of bills, cooking and cleaning. They lived for the salvation and good of all, with no financial gain for anyone – so those in the workshops had the time for the steady pursuit of excellence without the burden of worrying about economic survival. Following the advice of their founder, Mother Ann Lee, they worked as if they had 1,000 years to live, and as if they knew they were to die to-morrow. Their satisfaction was a job well done for its own sake. Shakers saw their skills as gifts from God, "Put your hands to work and your hearts to God" exhorted Mother Ann – and so the making of anything became a spiritual experience.

Many Shaker pieces were refinements of the everyday items the founders had used for many years in their native England. A classic example is the wooden oval box, universally recognized as an icon of Shaker quality, which was based on a box design that had been made in Europe for over 100 years. The Shakers simply refined it to the elegant proportions that became their trademark. The body of the box was made of pliable quartersawn maple, shaped around a form, while the tops and bottoms were of more stable pine, which was less likely than maple to bow up and pull away from the sides in damp winter weather.

The fluted lip around this prettily punched wall sconce protects the flame from draughts. This handcrafted design in tin has been given an antiqued finish.

The characteristic finger-like joins, known as swallowtail projections, allowed the maple to swell and shrink with changes in temperature and humidity, so the box was less likely to buckle than if it had a straight join. The Shakers elongated the swallowtails to more elegant proportions, and cut them with a knife instead of a saw, so as to bevel their edges. They pinned them into place with perfect lines of tacks made from copper, which would not discolour the wood. This detailing was the epitome of the Shaker saying "Trifles make perfection, but perfection itself is no trifle".

Charming in its simplicity, this tin lantern was an efficient lamp. The sides protected the flame from draughts, while reflecting and magnifying the light.

The pattern for Shaker baskets was borrowed from another culture – the Algonquin Indians. Instead of weaving whole, unsplit lengths of willow in the way that Mother Ann Lee's native English craftspeople would have done, these indigenous Americans made splints of wood to create a flatter weave. The Shakers adapted the methods, creating elegant curved and domed designs from what was a rugged prototype. During the 18th and 19th centuries, the Shakers made an industry of basket-making, supplying their handiwork throughout settled America. Their baskets are regarded today as among the finest splint baskets ever made.

Decorative Tinware

In the world outside the Shaker community, other groups of early American settlers also sought ways to make utility household items more attractive. However, without the benefits of communal living, there was less time for the meditative craftsmanship required to produce near-perfect forms, so their methods were generally decorative.

One example of this was tinware, which became much more refined at the beginning of the 18th century, after Paul Revere perfected a way to roll sheet metal, producing a finer material than the spun or stamped variety. Wall sconces, trinket boxes, candle holders, and panels for food safes were all made from tin, and often simply but effectively decorated with patterns of punched holes using a hammer and nail punch. The designs ranged from the child-like simplicity of concentric circles, squares and diamonds to more elaborate compositions, incorporating motifs from the makers' European roots. Hearts, flowers, birds, and baskets were popular, sometimes produced in outline, sometimes given fill-in and texture with closely punched holes.

Other tinware, such as jugs, coffee pots, trays, and tins was japanned to imitate Oriental lacquerware. First, the piece was given a layer of dark paint, often black, but sometimes vermilion, which was then painted – either freehand or using stencils – with brightly coloured birds, flowers and fruits. Family tin shops, known as whitesmiths (in contrast to their heavier-duty counterparts, blacksmiths, who dealt in sooty iron) were set up all along the Eastern seaboard. The pieces, which were generally made by the menfolk and decorated by the women, were sold on to pedlars, who would ply their way southward in a round trip that could be up to 1,000 miles or 1,600 kilometres. Some enterprising whitesmiths would head south and set up shop for a few months to supply the pedlars for their return journey.

Weathervanes – Street Sculpture

Folk art also had a place outdoors, in the form of weathervanes. These were essential in the early days, when folk were more reliant on the weather and there were no official forecasts. Weathervanes were cut from metal or carved from wood in simple silhouette. Often made by the craftsmen who also made trade signs, they were soon elevated to the status of local sculpture, taking on more detailed form, and, in the case of wood, careful colouring in polychrome for protection.

The choice of image often reflected the use of the building. A farmer, for example, may have chosen a rooster, cow or horse. In seaside settlements mermaids, sea serpents, sailors, whales and ships predominated. Indians were also popular, partly because their arrows made perfect pointers to the direction of the wind, and partly because in some country districts, they were used to indicate that the land had been bought from Indians, keeping away other bands, who may have assumed the land was rightfully theirs.

A dapper black and white duck is Pennsylvanian S R White's interpretation of an authentic decoy. The charm lies in the unique quality of each bird. Even today decoy ducks are still handmade.

Developing Decoys

Another form of folk art sculpture, popular even today, is decoy-making. But the tradition of these highly decorative works is rooted in the most basic need – hunting for food. The idea was borrowed from the indigenous Indians, who discovered that birds of a feather do indeed flock together, and can be lured within shooting range by craftily positioned models of their own kind. The original Indian versions, crudely made from heaps of mud and bunches of leaves, were surprisingly effective, but the settlers soon improved the prototypes by carving them into more believable shapes.

The style depended on the breed of the bird. Some small shore birds needed to be seen in full profile, so they were mounted on sticks, known as stickups, while waterbirds, such as ducks and geese, responded to floating decoys. At the other end of the scale, some decoys were more stylized, with fowl assembled from pieces of driftwood, string and nails. Once carved, the decoys were often painted. Some were given hasty symbolic markings, and although these were usually found to attract the prey much better than the more lifelike models, many makers prided themselves on meticulously painting in every feather.

Decoy-making still has a great following. Because they are inspired by a rudimentary Indian idea, rather than coming from European roots, many connoisseurs would go as far as to say they are the only true American Settler folk art form.

THE ART OF THE NEEDLE

The hours women spent working with needle and thread in centuries past resulted in the flowering of some of the most creative and fascinating works of folk art. These tell stories of the lives of their creators, giving us an insight into their philosophies. From a young age, girls had to learn all manner of stitchery, so they could make and mend clothes, linens and bedding, and were able to mark everything with embroidered initials. Tedious hours at school, spent labouring over the perfecting of these skills, were rewarded later when they could be used creatively to work exquisite embroideries and bedding, in one of the few creative outlets of their hard-working lives.

Sampler Simplicity

The first piece of a girl's creative stitchery was likely to be a sampler – probably an alphabet, together with her name and a date – worked in cross-stitch on a piece of linen. Subsequent samplers would include simple unshaded motifs that reflected the fashions of the time. In the 18th century, samplers often had religious overtones. However, after the French Revolution religious symbolism was banned in France, and French needlewomen began to stitch more everyday objects into their work. Houses, animals, vases of flowers and bowls of fruit began to appear in French needlework, along with cockerels and peacocks, which were usually given a border of stylized flowers or trellises.

As work from France spread abroad, it influenced needlewomen in other countries, and these motifs began to appear in their samplers and other work. Generally, girls made up their own designs, choosing motifs, alphabets and borders offered by the teacher, and then arranging them around their name, a date, or perhaps a verse from the Bible. Later in life, young women sometimes stitched samplers to commemorate an event such as a birth or betrothal.

The charm of these cross-stitched samplers is their child-like simplicity: the two-dimensional representational shapes; the sometimes quaint proportions; the insight lent by the chosen verses. Since it is the naïve quality of antique samplers that is the very essence of their appeal, it is not difficult to design your own. There are endless books that offer patterns for borders, alphabets and motifs. Or you can incorporate your own motifs, drawing them first on graph paper.

Cream and white fabrics displayed quilters' skills to greatest effect. They would execute intricate patterns in tiny, handmade stitches.

Geometric Patchwork

Quilt-making is another testament to the importance of folk art. As well as a thrifty means of night-time protection against the winter cold, quilts provide a record of an era: a little history, a little insight into a people was stitched into every top.

Quilts consist of three layers: a top; an insulating wadding of wool or cotton (though nowadays, synthetic equivalents are often used); and a backing. All are top-stitched together, either by hand with tiny running stitches, or, more recently, by machine. The stitching sometimes appears in straight lines, sometimes in intricate patterns. Generally, the plainer the quilt the more elaborate the quilting, and vice versa. The tops are at once the most interesting and most beautiful part of a quilt. The sheer expense of fabrics in the days before mass production necessitated the stitching together of tiny scraps of fabric, gleaned from worn-out clothes and bedlinen, to make a rich patchwork cloth.

Patchwork was no innovation, even a few centuries ago. Paintings dating back to the time when Rameses III ruled Egypt, between 1200 and 1168 BC, suggest the use of patchwork. But for centuries it was seen as utility and, as the patchworks wore and disintegrated, so they were perhaps used as stuffing for the next quilt, leaving few early records. But when the idea of patchwork was introduced to North America by the English, probably around the early part of the 18th century, quilts were transformed into an art form. In Pennsylvania especially, the German communities interpreted patchwork to suit their own, often religious philosophies, to stunning effect. Even the simplest one-patch quilts, with squares in carefully chosen colours arranged neatly side by side, could become an exquisite visual family history when made up of fabric scraps collected over generations.

More elaborate patchworks used a variety of different shapes – triangles, diamonds, hexagons, octagons, pentagons, arranged together to form blocks of patterns. These were given evocative names such as "Storm at Sea", "Mariner's Compass",

A modern appliqué takes inspiration from the Shaker motto: "Hearts to God and Hands to Work".

"Flying Geese", "Bear's Tracks", and "Log Cabin", or the more religious "Crown of Thorns", "Joseph's Coat" and "Jacob's Ladder", witness both to the roots of each community and the tough lives the people led.

Once all the blocks needed to make the quilt had been completed they were arranged into an overall design and stitched together. This offered ample opportunity for elaborate finished patchworks and made handling easier while work was in progress. The blocks may have been composed of four, five, six, or many more pieces. The more components in each block, the more accurate the cutting and stitching of each piece had to be, otherwise the design became distorted at the outer edges. The supreme test of skill in patchworking was to tackle a patchwork that featured a large central block made of many pieces – such as a sunburst or a pieced star in which sometimes hundreds of tiny diamonds were meticulously cut out and carefully stitched together.

Curvaceous Appliqué

Many quilt tops were appliquéd: fabric motifs were stitched to a background cloth to make an elaborate overall design. Sometimes, appliqué was used on its own, but it was more often used in conjunction with patchwork. Appliqué allowed for a break away from the strictly geometric patchwork designs favoured by the stricter religious sects, giving room for more sensuous curvy motifs – such as flowers, leaves and hearts – that often harked back to European roots. Many of the motifs carried religious symbolism relevant to the more moderate reformed groups. To them, lilies were a symbol of purity and the Virgin Mary; flowers represented Christ; the Rose of Sharon alluded to the Old Testament Song of Solomon; and stars were often called "The Star of Bethlehem" or "Star of the East".

Amish Purity

In sharp contrast to this elaborate decoration, the early Amish people with their strictly puritan ideals shunned all forms of decoration, from the use of printed fabric (unless it was used as a backing, hidden from view) to any kind of appliqué with its curved forms. Even the use of too many pieces was frowned on, lest the finished piece become a source of pride. But these restraints have left us with a rich legacy of quilts of extraordinary beauty consisting of large squares, triangles and rectangles in plain, though often bright, colours, all the more intensified by the popular use of a black background.

Closeted from the outside world, the Amish were not influenced by the current quilting fashions, so they had to rely on their own sense of design. With little to inspire them in their spartan homes, they resorted to everyday items for ideas. Some of the classic Amish designs bore a remarkable resemblance to the hymnals they brought from their German homelands, with square brass bosses in the corners and central brass diamonds.

As some groups of Amish began to move away, often to form less conservative religious communities, so their quilts became more vibrant. Heading west to Ohio, Indiana, Iowa, Illinois, and Missouri, they began to interact more with the outside world, and their quilts came to reflect this. The colours became more vibrant, the pieces smaller, and patterns and blocks were incorporated. Occasionally Amish women would even appliqué a central motif into their quilt, which would have been taboo back home.

While the piecing of an Amish quilt is traditionally very simple, and usually done by machine to create perfect sharp corners, the quilting, which was done by hand, was among the most intricate found in America. They would aim for 20 stitches to the inch/2.5 centimetres (almost impossible nowadays, if you use synthetic, rather than woollen fillings), working the whole quilt in finely executed designs. It is interesting that these designs were often in the form of leaves, flowers, feathers, tulips, wreaths, stars, trellises, and baskets – motifs that were almost identical to those used for appliqué by the less puritan Pennsylvanian sects. Bearing testimony to their European roots, the Amish perhaps justified this embellishment by using discreet matching threads for the quilting to keep the patterning subtle.

Quilting Detail

Common to many northern Americans, of any religious sect, quilt-making became an important part of a girl's life from an early age. The skills were learned at school, and girls were expected to complete one cover a year, piecing the top over winter, ready for quilting in the spring. The finished article would then be put away toward a dowry, usually numbering 12 quilts. The 13th, which would be complete when she was about 21, was generally held to be the bridal quilt.

In North America, quilting was a communal job. Women would gather at a quilting bee, and aim to have the cover stitched together by the end of the day. Even the children would lend a hand, threading needles for a penny a go. Quilting bees were often combined with a barn raising (which the men would tackle), or some other celebration. When a girl invited friends to quilt her 13th cover (the bridal quilt), she was also inviting them to her engagement party.

Another reason for getting together for the finishing was that the making of the whole quilt was often a communal effort. Sometimes all the women in the community would each make a block to be sewn into what was known as an Album or Presentation quilt. This would be given as a gift to a bride or a respected member of the community such as a minister or a

A contemporary one-patch quilt in coordinating prints demonstrates how simplicity can be inspired by the intricacies of yesteryear to great effect.

nurse. A young man might be given a Freedom presentation quilt on his 21st birthday, and a family moving away a Friendship presentation quilt with each block signed by its maker.

Such fast-track quilting probably had its roots in the early settler days when there was a great need to provide winter warmth in a hurry. In those days, quilts were used as underblankets and curtains, as well as bedcovers, and many were needed for each family. Communal quilting certainly contrasted with the English practice. There, quilting was a craft to be carried out with pride by both men and women. Quilters either took work into their homes or travelled from farm to farm, staying on the premises until the job was done. They were jealous of their own personal styles and would not have wanted anyone to lend a hand.

A small cream bear, clutching a bag of cinnamon sticks, makes a charming gift.

TIME FOR TOYS

It is hard to imagine, given the hard work simply to survive in the last century, that there was any time left for making toys. But toymaking has always had a special place in traditional crafts, appealing both to children and to the child in the adult. Children prefer simplicity, often choosing the symbolic rather than the realistic, allowing space for their imagination. This lends a freedom to the makers – and it goes a long way to explaining the appeal of handmade toys. The uneven features on a doll's face simply add character.

Rag Dolls

Unless you are handy with the jigsaw and plane, probably the easiest toys to make at home are rag dolls. Little girls everywhere love their soft huggable bodies and, with their hand-stitched faces, each one has a personality of its own. Simple, removable clothes add to the enjoyment for the child.

The most famous rag doll in recent history, Raggedy Ann, not only spawned a million lookalikes, but became the heroine of a series of children's books. Her story is a poignant one, that even today seems to bring her alive. The original Raggedy Ann must go back to the early part of the last century, because she was found in an attic in 1914 by her original owner's great grand daughter, Marcella Gruelle. Thrilled by her discovery, Marcella took the worn and faceless rag doll to her artist writer father, Johnny, who revived it by sewing on two button eyes, drawing in a triangular nose, a smile, and a heart on her chest, under which he inscribed "I love you". Marcella named her Raggedy Ann after the characters in James's Whitcombe's poems – Raggedy Man and Orphan Annie. Sadly, Marcella died just three years afterwards, but she will be remembered through the Raggedy Ann Stories which her father subsequently wrote and illustrated.

Wooden Toys

Folk rag dolls really only date back to the last century, because before that the cost of cloth made them prohibitively expensive. Earlier, most folk dolls and other toys were whittled from wood, a tradition that goes back to prehistory. Those early dolls were not playthings – they were often mystical figures used for religious purposes. However, there are references to dolls used as toys in early Greek and Roman literature. These had almost disappeared by medieval times – perhaps because children were expected to contribute their share of chores to the household and had no time for dolls. Perhaps, also, dolls were shunned by religious groups for being too like graven images. Certainly, until recently Amish girls had to make do with a stick or a bottle wrapped in a blanket for a doll. And even when the Amish did start to sew dolls, they were forbidden to sew features on their faces, which were left blank.

In Europe, the modern tradition for doll-making dates back to 15th-century Nuremburg, which later became the toy-making centre of the world. From 1700, dolls were carved in wood and painted in a style that was copied all over Europe and influenced the German settlers in North America.

In 18th-century England, hand-carved and painted Queen Anne dolls became very popular. They were made both at home and by craftsmen. Each one had an individual, hand-made charm. This was not seen on the continent of Europe, where trades guilds dictated that carvers should pass the dolls on to specialist painters. Later, intricately jointed wooden peg dolls, also known as Dutch dolls (a corruption of Deutsch) were imported in their thousands from Germany. Their main feature, which has endured right up to the present day, is the painted-on, centrally parted black hair, a style typical of the mid-19th century.

A simple form of these dolls has been copied even by children, who used to paint the top knob of a wooden clothes peg with facial features and the characteristic hairstyle, then

This simple rag doll, complete with a huge heart on her chest, has been dressed in traditional Shaker homespun fabrics.

dressed the "doll" using fabric scraps. Records in an 1895 women's magazine show a slightly more elaborate and certainly more fashionable "Clothespin Doll", complete with full instructions on how to make elaborate crêpe paper dresses trimmed with lace and tulle.

American chequerboards were often decorated with paintings, a tradition probably originated by tavern sign writers supplementing their income with smaller sidelines. This one, crackle glazed for antique effect, is made by Barbara Wagaman from Pennsylvania.

Ephemeral Toys

Dolls have always been made from whatever is around. Farm children may have made horticultural dolls – a magazine article from 1869 suggests making one from an upside-down hollyhock flower with straw arms, and a head of grapes topped with corn silk hair.

Other ephemeral dolls, loved down the ages, are paper cutouts. These were sold on sheets along with cutout clothes. Victorian magazines exhorted children to make their own dolls from "Bristol Board" mounted on a wire stand, and then gave patterns for elaborate frocks and hats. Sometimes it was suggested that adjustments be made to give the doll more lifelike proportions, so that women could use the dressed doll as a model for their dressmakers. This harks back to 18th-century France, when couturiers made life-size or half-size dolls, which were dressed in the latest samples and sent all around Europe to display the latest fashions. These were called "dolls of the Rue St Honoré", which was the Parisian dressmaking centre. As paper and printing became cheaper toward the end of the 19th century, these were replaced by paper figures with printed paper costumes.

Moving Toys and Whirligigs

Toys that move have always been popular, and toy-makers down the centuries have striven to introduce movement by jointing dolls' limbs, transforming them into puppets; by adding wheels, and by employing more complicated techniques. Whirligigs, which are a form of tabletop weather vane, are a fine example of this. Such toys fall into two categories: articulated dolls in many forms; and windmill types. The simplest ones, like weathervanes, simply have propeller-type arms that spin the figure as the wind blows. This developed into an art form as whirligigs became more complex – with propellers, gears and rods that made figures ride bicycles, chop wood, or milk cows. They were often put in front of a house, on a fence, there to carry out their designated activity, gently or wildly depending on the weather. In religious communities, this was one toy allowed for the Sabbath, presumably to give time for meditation and contemplation.

Another toy allowed for the Sabbath was a Noah's Ark, because of its association with the Bible. This was fortunate, since wooden animals have always been a favourite theme for home-made toys. Most homes had a Noah's Ark, complete with pairs of exotic animals from far-off lands copied from book illustrations. Sabbath was also the day that sailors and fishermen are thought to have made toys, many of which they whittled from whales' teeth, or scrimshaw as it was known.

Game Boards

In the days before radio and television, long evenings needed to be filled with games. Classic games like chess, backgammon, draughts and noughts and crosses (tic-tac-toe), have been played for centuries in communities all around the world. Each developed a different style of game board, often finely finished and painted or inlaid with ebony, ivory or tooled leather.

In North America, game boards provided an opportunity for sign painters and hobby artists to display their skills. As well as the simple chequered design necessary for the play area, many were decorated with much more than a simple border design. Larger portions of the board – perhaps the top half, or a quarter above and a quarter below the squares – were given over to decorative space in which to place dispensed-with pieces during the game. The decoration could be anything from a few simple motifs to a stylized landscape, typical of the painting style of the time, or a single image such as a cockerel or a sunrise, similar to those that may have been seen on tavern signs. This gives rise to the idea that these decorative boards made useful sidelines for itinerant signwriters who were a little low on commissions.

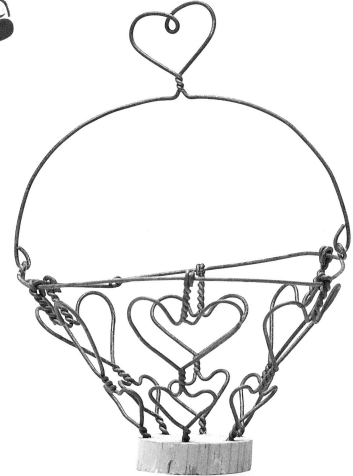

Wire, twisted into heart shapes and fixed into a wooden base, makes a delightful hanging basket.

The chequered part of the design lends these simple but beautiful examples of folk art a graphic quality that is easy to reproduce authentically, yet the boards offer space for modern-day crafters to express themselves in their own style.

WELCOME HOME

From time immemorial people the world over have wanted to make their home their own. It has never mattered how small or how temporary the home was – think of the cramped proportions of traditional gypsy caravans, which were, nevertheless, richly furnished with flamboyantly decorated artefacts, and draped with elaborate fabrics; or the European barge folk,

who plied their ways around the canals of Europe in brightly decorated vessels, using tin utensils extravagantly painted in bright colours on black. The nomads of Arabia also had a rich tradition in their dwellings. Once the tents had been pitched on new desert sites, intricately designed rugs and carpets were laid out to make that place a home.

Somehow, the fewer resources there are around the more resourceful people have to be. This was certainly true of the early American settlers, who brought very little with them from their European homelands, but carried in their imaginations all the visual influences they had left behind, which they tapped for ideas for decorating their new homes. Until consumer goods became readily available, generations of Americans had to rely on their own resources and skills to create all the necessities for living, along with any kind of decoration to enrich their lives.

Each group developed its own style, depending on religious beliefs and its members' homeland. The Shakers, whose leader, Mother Ann Lee, came from Manchester, England, espoused a devout belief that shunned all embellishment, and developed the equivalent of modern minimalism. Furnishings were sparse; decoration absent. Without the distraction of pattern, focus was thrown on to form, providing a discipline of perfection.

The Pennsylvanian Germans also left their homelands for religious reasons. Some, like the Mennonites and the Amish, also shunned fancy decoration, though their style was far less monastic than that of the Shakers, allowing at least colour, if not pattern. Other groups, like the Lutherans and other Reformed sects, came mainly from the weaving centres of Germany and Switzerland, bringing with them a rich visual dictionary, which influenced the decoration of their homes, furniture and textiles. This was overlaid with what they were able to accomplish, plus current influences being imported from Europe.

Whitesmiths fashioned tin into shapes, while their womenfolk painted them in bright shapes reminiscent of European bargeware.

Wall Stencils

The early American homes often had a simple charm, born of the fact that each community did not necessarily have skilled craftsmen of every type. As the communities became more established, there was time to add decoration in a style that has come to be seen as distinctly Pennsylvanian. Their highly decorative, stencilled walls must be one of the most dramatic examples of this. Sometimes elaborate, sometimes simple designs in mellow reds, greens and yellows were applied to backgrounds of plaster tinted white, pink, yellow, gray, light green or light blue. The colours were hand-mixed using local clays and brick dust mixed with skimmed milk, creating tones that naturally sympathized with their surroundings.

The tradition for decorating walls is rooted in Europe of the 17th century, when a painter known as François of Rouen began to stencil lengths of paper to mimic the tapestries hanging in aristocratic French houses. The idea travelled to England, and on to the Bay Colony. Paper stainers used to stencil and later print patterns on to paper sheets measuring 56 by 86 centimetres/22 by 32 inches, though soon, 11-metre/12-yard lengths were sold on rolls.

However, by the time these costly papers had been shipped, they were prohibitively expensive for all but a few, so the idea of stencilling straight on to the walls was born. Itinerant of craftsmen would travel the area, decorating people's houses – and, at the same time, developing a folk art of their own. The intricate European designs proved to be too difficult and costly to reproduce, so the stencillers simplified the designs, further adding to their charm.

The arrangement of the stencils on the wall followed the conventions of wallpapering, with vertical bands of simple motifs separating panels of more complex designs. Very often, an elaborate focus design was applied over a mantelpiece, and borders were added at ceiling and skirting-board level. The motifs were influenced by the original settlers' roots in southern Germany and Switzerland, so that they brought with them their own folk symbolism. Hearts and bells meant joy, pine-apples hospitality, and the willow, which was often seen in mourning pictures, symbolized immortality.

Floorings

Originally, floor-covering was no more than a rudimentary scattering of sand on to boards, but as life became easier for the settlers, floorboards, like walls, were stencilled, usually with designs mimicking tiles or rugs. Alternatively, the boards were left plain and covered with colourfully decorated floor-cloths made from canvas strengthened with linseed oil paint. Rag rugs were also used to "carpet" floorboards. As their name suggests, these were made from torn-up rags that were then either made into long plaits and coiled into a mat, or cut up and hooked into canvas for a looped rug effect.

Dower chests were typically decorated in panels, the number of panels depending on the size of the chest. German-style symbolic flowers in vases were a popular motif.

Overmantels and Fireboards

Sometimes, in place of a stencilled feature over the mantelpiece, a family would commission a painting. These were very often landscapes, usually painted by itinerant artists, who, while they were about it, may have painted the fireboard too. Fire-boards, used to seal off the fireplace in the summer, were wide wooden boards cut to fit the opening and held together with battens. It was commonplace to have them scenically decorated or painted with animals or vases of flowers.

Decorative Furniture

In country homes, furniture was painted, usually to disguise the plain softwood maple and pine it was made from. Some-times, trompe l'oeil techniques were used to imitate the elegant hardwoods used by the English furniture makers of the time, such as Hepplewhite and Sheraton. Techniques for applying colour were developed, using sponges, rags, crumpled news-

Fruits and birds were typical subject matter of Victorian theorem paintings, which were executed using stencils carefully arranged into a pleasing composition. This modern one is by Hope Angier of Wiscasset, Maine.

papers, and feathers – a rich inheritance that is now enjoying renewed popularity.

Much more popular in 19th-century America was country furniture that had been colourfully painted and decorated. Simple cupboards, chests, chairs, tables, and even clocks were embellished with scripts and symbolic motifs rooted in the German homeland. Lilies symbolized the Madonna, and purity; tulips, with their three upstanding petals, the Trinity; the half-fish Mermaid represented the half-human, half-divine Christ; and unicorns were considered the guardians of virginity. This type of decoration is still popular today.

Dower Chests

One of the richest sources of Pennsylvanian folk art of this kind is found on dower chests, which were presented to women on the occasion of their betrothal, to hold the household linens, samplers and quilts that would become their dowry. Some families made and decorated these themselves, others employed a local carpenter to make the chest, which was then painted by an itinerant decorator or Fractur artist who would have added names, dates and inscriptions. Each region developed its own style. Lancaster County's distinctive look incorporated pale painted arched panels featuring elaborate motifs. The central panel often featured a male figure to represent the groom.

Popular Art

The walls of early American homes were hung with paintings of a distinctive style. Because they were usually painted by artists with little or no training, they did not display accurate proportions or perspectives, sophisticated compositions or atmospheric lighting, but they had a naïve quality all of their own. Full face portraits and landscapes were popular. Although few artists were trained, many were professional, in that they travelled around painting all manner of things – tavern and shop signs, portraits and landscapes, walls and furniture.

Ironically, many of the American folk painters who did have training were not professional, in the sense that they did not earn a living from their art. These were middle class young ladies, who were sent to finishing school from about the 1830s to study, among other subjects, painting and composition.

It is indicative of the rigorous life in centuries past that it was considered an essential part of a young lady's education to learn how to make a Mourning Picture. These were often composed on velvet, using paint, needlework, scraps of fabric, and lace. Most included funeral motifs, such as mourners, willow trees, and urns, and often a church in the background.

A somewhat cheerier form of folk art was the Theorem Painting, which was made using stencils. It would probably be more accurate to call these compositions, as the women would cut their own stencils – often of extremely simple shapes such as fruits, trees, butterflies, and birds, and arrange them into a picture. The same shapes were used again and again to make different compositions. A good theorem painting showed skilled shading in the colour and careful penning of details, executed once the colours had dried. It was a clever system that could produce excellent results, giving everyone the chance to make a beautiful picture.

CELEBRATIONS

Celebrations are the stuff of life's memories; the punctuation marks that highlight the special times against the humdrum background of life's routines. There is a basic human need, whatever our circumstances, to highlight our lives with festivities, annually commemorating the passing of the seasons, or marking the rites of passage – the birth of a baby, the enrolment into adulthood, a marriage, a retirement. These days we still celebrate, but our greetings are sent on bought cards; personal details recorded only on impersonal printed forms; and memories are stored in the family photograph album or on a video. In centuries past, heartfelt greetings and precious records all had to be executed by hand, and so were saved for the most special occasions and the dearest of friends and relatives, who treasured them as keepsakes.

Elegant Calligraphy

Beautifully scripted handwriting is admired nowadays as much, or maybe even more than it always was. But in the days before typewriters, even records and business correspondence had to be executed by hand, so good writing was paramount. Many hours were spent teaching children the art of calligraphy (literally "beautiful writing"), as a good hand was seen as a mark of education and culture.

In America during the 19th century, a schoolmaster, Platt Rogers Spencer, evolved a writing style that he had published as a manual for teaching penmanship in schools and business academies. Pupils learned a series of strokes – curved and straight, broad and fine, light and heavy – that were translated into the letters of the alphabet. This was taken a stage further by using those same strokes to create decorative illustrations.

Birds and animals were popular subjects for these drawings, because the use of calligraphic curves was an accomplished way of showing movement. A bold sweep across the page became a bird in flight; finely traced flourishes the vanes of feathers. These illustrations were finished with a wash of watercolour and used to embellish writings. Sometimes, the illustrations and the script were worked on separate pieces of paper, to be cut out and arranged into an elegant composition on another sheet. Here, then, were the ingredients of greetings cards made and sent even by schoolchildren in the last century.

The Art of Fractur

Special documents, such as certificates of birth, baptism or marriage deserved particular attention, and these were the occasions when among the German-speaking communities, the Fractur artist would be employed. Fractur writing, a style of illuminated manuscript brought to America by German immigrants, was originally worked by members of religious communities. It had its roots in the hand-written illuminated works of medieval Europe, and, by tradition, was rarely signed, so as to emulate the work of clerical scribes of centuries past.

Although Fractur was dying out in Europe, 19th-century America saw it flourishing into a folk art used to decorate all manner of things, as well as to illuminate documents, song books and bookmarks. Dower chests and furniture, even walls were inscribed. And some of the stricter religious sects would commission Fractur to hang on the wall in place of portraits, which were prohibited by their faith. Church ministers and schoolmasters began to take on manuscript work, and as the demand grew, bands of itinerant Fractur artists would travel the land, accepting commissions for almost anything that could be commemorated, including family records or even a seasonal blessing.

Illuminated manuscripts, called Fractur, were used for all manner of certificates in 18th- and 19th-century Pennsylvania. This one, by Robert Miller from Maine, is made in the traditional manner.

Moving away from the original clerical influence, Fractur drawing and painting predictably grew more flamboyant and often less sophisticated because many of the artists were not trained. While early examples were finely executed and given subtle illustrative decoration with delicately coloured illuminations, later ones showed more vibrantly toned illustrations that took up a greater and greater proportion of the work, in some cases replacing the script altogether.

Intricate Papercuts

Before the age of mass production, when greetings had to be handmade, even some of the less important celebrations, such as birthdays, Valentines and seasonal festivities took on a more commemorative tone than they do today. If time and effort had to be put into making cards, there was sense in designing them to be kept, or even framed and hung on the wall. This is perhaps how paper-cutting developed from a simple childhood activity into a skill.

There is something beguiling about snipping simple shapes from folded paper which then unfolds in a pattern of perfect symmetry. This was transformed into an art form in 18th-century Switzerland, where black or white paper was scissored and scalpelled into intricate images incorporating delicate trellises, stylized trees with fine feathery leaves, urns, birds, animals, and flowers. In Poland, paper-cutting became a popular art, though the preference there was to build layer upon layer of papercuts into a collage, sometimes painting the motifs for extra depth. These traditions were transported to North America by the early settlers, who have left a legacy of finely cut and painted masterpieces.

The fascination for the fine cutting of paper could well have been fired by the late 18th-century/early 19th-century enthusiasm for silhouette-cutting. These profile portraits, originally cut from black paper, were popularized by those who could not afford to have a painted likeness. Silhouettes became such a craze in America by the 1820s that they spawned hundreds of professionals and thousands of amateurs, all of whom were extremely deft with scissors and paper.

Decking the Halls

Celebration has always called for the temporary decoration of homes in honour of the festivity. With no available ready-made ornamentation, the only option in the last century was to make use of everyday items and materials in what was often a more honest and sympathetic display. Arrangements of natural and often seasonal materials fitted happily into their surroundings, lending fragrant as well as decorative appeal. So at harvest time and Thanksgiving, freshly picked apples and pears offered a honeyed sweetness, while dried herbs and spices, such as bay, cloves and cinnamon gave Christmas a pungent warmth.

Wire bent into various shapes, then threaded with cranberries and decorated with fir and fabric scraps, make for original decorations.

From Elizabethan times, smaller fragrant decorations, such as pomanders, were popular. To make these, oranges were stuck with cloves and were preserved by allowing them to dry out slowly. When they were ready, they were arranged in bowls or hung on ribbons to be grouped into a display. The perfume was revived over the Christmas festivities with the occasional splashing of hot or boiling water.

Smaller festive decorations for hanging on trees and at windows were made from whatever was at hand. In Germany, many were cooked. Delicious biscuity *Lebkuchen* (life cakes), spiced with cinnamon and ginger, were cut into the shapes of stars, hearts, bells and birds and threaded with ribbon for hanging, as were larger gingerbread hearts decorated with messages in icing. Salt dough was fashioned into simple and elaborate shapes, then glazed and baked so it could be kept for subsequent years. Elsewhere, simple shapes made from available materials, such as punched tin or fabric scraps, were popular. At other times, dried herbs and slices of dried fruits or vegetables were threaded on to wire forms. For Christmas, popular shapes were stars, bells, hearts, and angels, plus fish – an ancient Christian icon.

At Easter, in many countries, it is traditional to decorate eggs, colouring them with natural dyes or using various techniques to pattern them. In Switzerland, young girls would tint eggs in glorious copper shades using a home-made dye prepared from onion skins. Sometimes they would make a mask using a spring leaf or flower before dyeing the egg so as to leave a seasonal imprint on the shell. The Swiss also engraved eggs, using a sharp knife to scratch a simple outline design of flora or fauna into the shell of a dyed egg.

In Poland and the Ukraine, the womenfolk used a batik method of wax-resist dyeing to produce intricately patterned eggs of many colours, all the more intensified by their traditionally black background. This art, known as Pisanki, travelled with immigrants to North America, where New England groups still make an annual ritual of elaborately decorating eggs in this way.

One of the less important celebrations, but one which is universally enjoyed, is St Valentine's day, when love tokens are secretly exchanged. Traditionally, all manner of cards were made – from intricate papercuts to collages of silk and lace. The "Heart in Hand", originally a religious symbol and indicative of love and piety, is sometimes used for Valentine cards. Some say the motif originates from the old English custom of a gentleman giving a glove to the woman of his choice on St Valentine's day.

A star-shaped Christmas decoration made in the same way as the heart shown opposite.

But whatever the past meanings, the Heart in Hand makes a symbolic Valentine card with an easy graphic shape that would look striking framed and hung on the wall . . . which, of course, continues the folk art tradition of keepsake cards.

MAKING THE USEFUL BEAUTIFUL

Shaker-style Bandbox

Oval boxes with a distinctive swallowtail join have become a signature of the style of the Shakers. This strict religious sect, an offshoot of the Quakers, permitted little decoration in their homes, so the beauty of these boxes lies in their functional simplicity. Boxes were made in all sizes for storing anything and everything in the home. Ladies travelling by stagecoach carried them as hand luggage. They were originally fashioned from wood – traditionally maple and pine – and were sometimes round, but oval is an easier shape to make.

In 18th-century England, bandboxes made from paper were popular for storing gentlemen's shirt collars. These three oval stacking boxes are made from card and papier mâché. They are useful for storing small objects – earrings or oddities.

1 Trace the templates (on page 34–5). Extend the side pieces by the appropriate measurements. Cut out the pattern pieces from card.

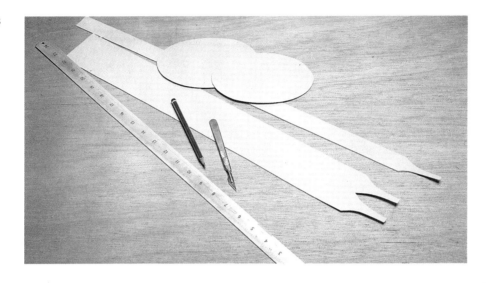

MATERIALS AND EQUIPMENT

◆ large sheet of pliable craft card

◆ a few sheets of newspaper

◆ masking tape

◆ double-sided tape

◆ scalpel

◆ metal ruler

◆ pencil

◆ gesso

◆ blue emulsion paint

◆ PVA glue

◆ 2.5cm/1in paintbrush

◆ bradawl

◆ small brass paper fasteners

◆ jar of wallpaper paste made up to a thick soupy consistency

2 Bend the side pieces to fit tightly around the base and lid, making sure the swallowtail shape matches at the front. Stick the overlap in place with double-sided tape. Use masking tape to fix the side pieces together on the inside.

3 Tear the sheets of newspaper into strips about 3–4cm/ 1¼–1½in wide. Coat the strips on both sides with wallpaper paste, then cover the card box inside and outside with two or three layers. Smooth out any air bubbles with your fingers, then use your thumbnail to define the swallowtail shape. Leave the box in a warm place to dry completely.

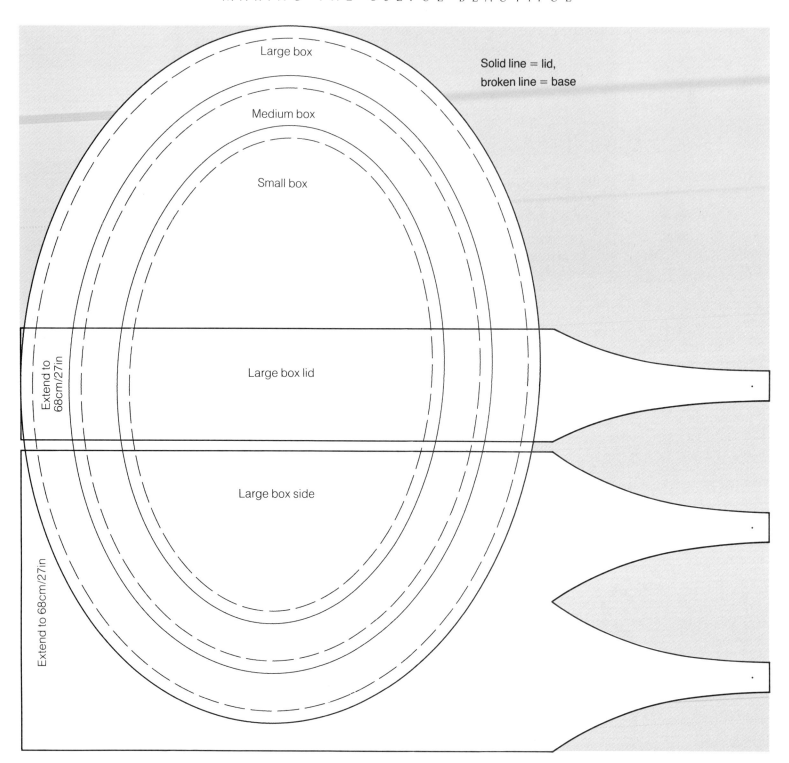

Large box

Medium box

Small box

Solid line = lid,
broken line = base

Extend to 68cm/27in

Large box lid

Large box side

Extend to 68cm/27in

MAKING THE USEFUL BEAUTIFUL

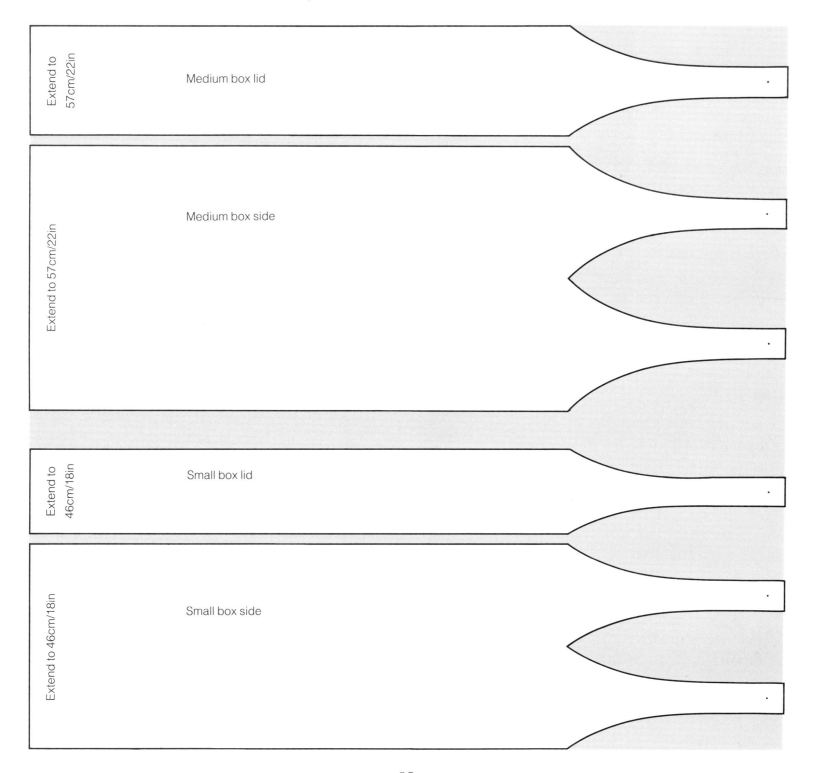

Extend to 57cm/22in

Medium box lid

Extend to 57cm/22in

Medium box side

Extend to 46cm/18in

Small box lid

Extend to 46cm/18in

Small box side

4 Coat the box with gesso. This is a quick-drying acrylic emulsion used to seal the paper and to cover the newsprint.

TIP

Paint the inside of the box and lid in a contrasting colour, or line with coloured or patterned fabric.

5 Cover the outside of the box with one or two coats of blue emulsion paint. Allow good drying time between coats. When the paint is dry, cover the paintwork with one coat of PVA glue to seal and protect the paint and to give a slight sheen.

6 Using a bradawl, pierce holes in the swallowtail overlaps where indicated on the pattern, and insert small brass paper fasteners. Open out the prongs of the fasteners on the inside.

Rag Rug

*Weaving old bits and pieces together to make floor coverings was a
way of making a home warmer and more comfortable in Europe for
centuries. The craft travelled across the Atlantic with the first settlers in
America – but because it was considered a working-class craft, not an
art, it was dismissed, and its development went unrecorded.
We know, however, that rag rugs have been made by two main
methods. Strips of fabric were tufted and prodded through a backing
fabric or plaited into lengths and coiled in concentric circles. This
colourful rug uses the last method. Make it from remnants of dress
fabric, worn bedlinen or old, lightweight curtains. Plait or braid
together strips of fabric, then stitch the plaits in a spiral, adding on
more plaits to make the rug the size you want.*

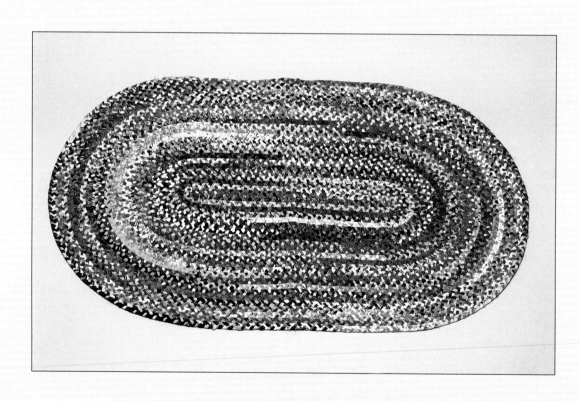

1 Cut each fabric into strips about 7cm/ 2¾in wide. Join the strips together to make 2m/6ft 6¾in lengths. Fold the raw edges to the centre, then use the safety pin to join the ends.

2 You will need to secure the safety pin to a hook or a nail in a wall or on your work surface. Plait or braid the fabric strips, folding in the raw edges as you go. Take care not to tangle the long ends of fabric.

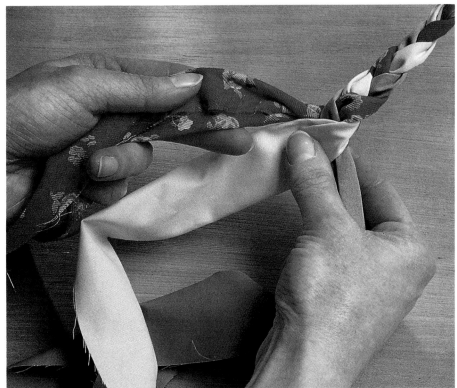

MATERIALS AND EQUIPMENT

◆ cotton fabric in three colours or patterns

◆ sharp scissors

◆ matching sewing thread

◆ sewing needle

◆ large safety pin

3 When you reach the end, trim and tack two ends together, then wrap the third end around it to enclose the raw edges. Stitch neatly in place. Finish the other end in the same way.

4 To begin making the rug, coil a plait, and stitch each row to the previous one on the wrong side. Join on new plaits by stitching the finished ends into the folds of fabric and stitching securely in place. Add on as many plaits as you like.

TIPS

Plait three strips of fabric of the same colour to add contrasting stripes or edging to your rug.

Sew on a fabric backing if the rug is to be used a lot.

Punched Tin Candle Sconces

German immigrants in Pennsylvania turned the new lightweight tin that became available during the 18th century to good use in their kitchens. Until then, cooking equipment was made from heavy iron, but the new rolled tin was strong, smooth, and light. Tinsmiths, called whitesmiths, fashioned sheets of tin into useful, lightweight kitchen implements – one whitesmith's range numbered 54 items. Thrifty homesteaders bought rolled tin and made things for themselves, turning a functional manufacturing process into a craft.

Punched tinwork turned useful candle sconces – which protected the flames from draughts and reflected their light back into the room – into decorative objects. Make these pretty candle sconces by recycling tin cans, which are thin enough to be easy to cut and shape. The perforations that form the pattern are made by tapping a metal centre punch into the tin. You can decorate old coffee tins with punched patterns. Just sand away any printing or paint, then punch in your design.

1 Remove the snap-on lid from the coffee tin and cut the tin in half with the tin snips. Cut off the base of the tin and open out and flatten the side piece.

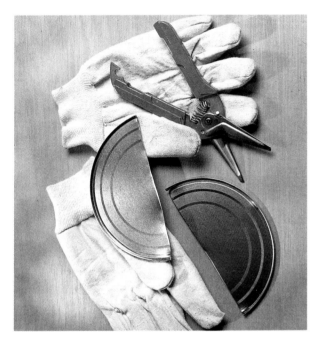

2 Trace and enlarge the pattern template. Cut out a basic sconce shape from the flattened tin sheet. Make small snips around the curved edge and bend back the little tabs you have formed using pliers. This will make the edge neat and safe.

MATERIALS AND EQUIPMENT

- large tin can (eg an old coffee tin)
- tin snips
- protective gloves
- tack hammer
- centre punch
- pliers
- tracing paper
- pencil
- masking tape
- thick card pad to protect your work surface
- small bulldog clips
- epoxy resin glue

Enlarge the template on a photocopier by 25%

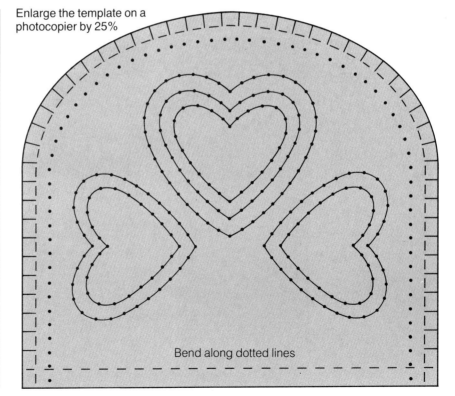

Bend along dotted lines

3 Trim the edge of the pattern to fit the back of the sconce, and hold it in place with masking tape. Protect your work surface with a thick card pad.

4 Place the back of the sconce flat on the card pad. Punch along the lines on the template using the centre punch and a tack hammer.

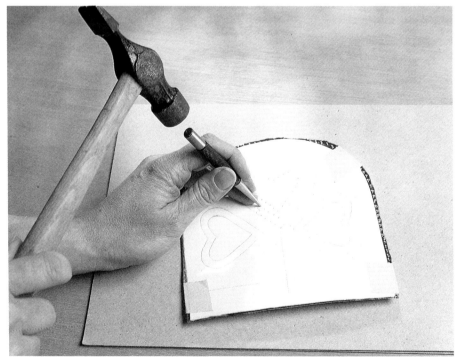

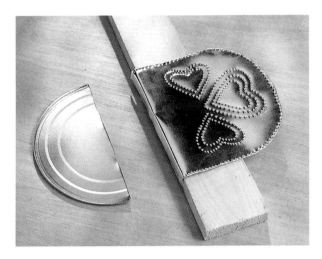

5 Bend the lower edge over a piece of wood to form a right angle.

6 Fix the sconce back to the base using a strong epoxy resin glue. Hold it in place with a few small bulldog clips.

SAFETY NOTE

Always use protective gloves when handling cut metal, as the edges are very sharp.

TIPS

Old tin cans are a good source of material for sconces. Cut off the base and lid with tin snips or a can opener, then cut down the centre seam and open out the side pieces.

Circular sconce

Use the base of the large tin as a back for the circular candle sconce. Punch a heart motif at the centre and around the base in concentric circles. Glue the back to a smaller can base to hold the candle.

Painted Tinware

Transform plain tin tea caddies or canisters with hand-painted floral motifs inspired by Pennsylvanian Dutch toleware. This colourful tableware made from sheet metal – usually tin – and painted, enamelled or lacquered, was popular in the homes of German settlers in Pennsylvania ("Dutch" is a corruption of "Deutsch"). Toleware was decorative. Jugs, coffee pots, trays, and containers were made to give as presents on special occasions. They were kept and rarely used, except for decoration and display – which is why so many examples have survived in beautiful condition, to be displayed in American museums today.

These brightly painted containers have a protective coating of varnish, so they can be safely used and washed.

1 Key the surface of the tea caddy with wet and dry sandpaper. Wipe it with a cloth soaked in white spirit to remove dust. Paint on two coats of matt black emulsion paint. Allow good drying time between coats following the instructions on the paint tin. Trace the floral design. Tape the traced design to a piece of chalk-backed carbon paper of the same size, then transfer the design to the tin. Tape the carbon paper to the tin and trace through the layers with a pencil.

Pattern for lid

Pattern for side of tin

MATERIALS AND EQUIPMENT

- tin tea caddy
- tracing paper
- chalk-backed carbon paper
- pencil
- low tack masking tape
- wet and dry sandpaper
- small paintbrushes
- 2.5cm/1in paintbrush
- matt black emulsion paint
- acrylic paints (red, green, blue, yellow, white and black)
- mixing palette
- clear varnish in a satin finish
- soft cloth and white spirit

2 Mix the basic base colours in a palette and apply them to each part of the design using a small paintbrush.

3 Lighten each colour with white paint, then add details and highlights to the basic design. Use our picture as a guide, or experiment with your own ideas.

TIP

Acrylic paints are very quick-drying and when dry they are permanent. They are ideal for use when you are handling the object you are painting, as they decrease the risk of smudging the design. Practise the brush strokes on a spare sheet of paper before decorating the tin, to accustom yourself to the flowing motion required.

4 When the paint is dry, lightly wipe over with a soft cloth soaked in white spirit to remove the chalk marks. Apply two coats of clear satin varnish with a 2.5cm/1in paintbrush, allowing good drying time between coats.

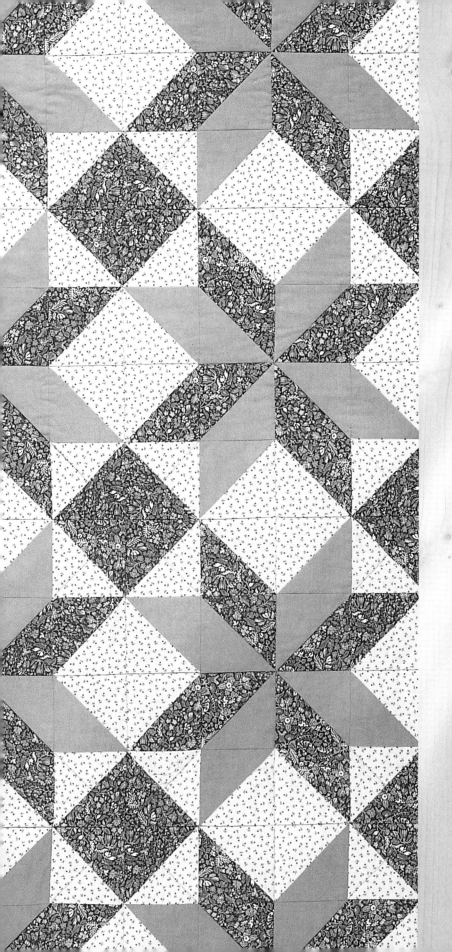

THE ART OF THE NEEDLE

Pieced Patchwork Cushion

Cushions are a modern application of a traditional craft. The farmsteads of hardworking American settlers were furnished with objects that were largely functional. Quilts were used to cover beds and windows at cold times of year, not to make soft places to sit; and pillows were often the only cushions in a home.

But the patchwork squares from which quilt patterns are made up are an ideal size for modern cushions, and the traditional patchwork patterns make striking cushion covers. Many of the classic quilt patterns were based on religious themes – the red cover on the right uses a traditional pattern called "Cross and Crown", commemorating Jesus and the crown of thorns. The green pattern on the left is called "Evening Star".

MATERIALS AND EQUIPMENT

Cross and Crown Cushion

- ◆ 51cm/20in of 112cm/44in-wide ivory fabric
- ◆ 30cm/12in of 112cm/44in-wide red spotted cotton fabric
- ◆ 10cm × 10cm/4in × 4in square red cotton fabric
- ◆ sewing needles and pins
- ◆ matching sewing thread
- ◆ sharp scissors
- ◆ sheet of plain pattern paper
- ◆ pencil and ruler
- ◆ 35cm/14in square cushion pad

Note: this cover fits a 35cm/14in cushion pad. Adjust pattern and fabric requirements accordingly if your cushion pad is larger or smaller.

DRAFTING THE PATTERN

You will see from the patchwork diagram that the 35cm/14in square pattern is divided into five equal parts along each side to form a grid of 25 squares. The squares can then be joined, divided or subdivided to form the pattern.

Most patchwork designs are made from squares with sides divided into 4, 5, 7 or 9 equal parts, and are thus called 4, 5, 7 or 9 "patch" designs. The variations are limitless, so why not use a traditional design as an inspiration to create your own patchwork using a blank grid?

1 Draw the pattern full size on a plain sheet of paper, cut out the basic pieces, numbers 1, 2, 3 and 4. Redraw these pieces, adding 1.5cm/⅝in seam allowance all round. Number the pattern pieces as indicated.

2 For the cushion backs, draw on to plain paper a rectangle two-thirds the depth of the cushion front, add 1.5cm/⅝in seam allowance all round.

Patch grid

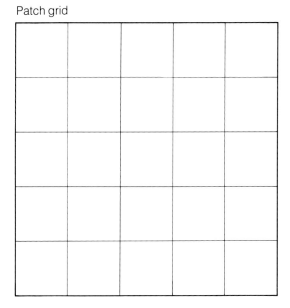

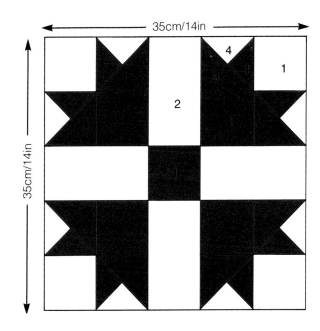

1 cut 4 red/4 white/1 plain red
2 cut 4 white
3 cut 4 red
4 cut 8 red/8 white

1 Cut out the fabric pieces accurately with sharp scissors. Pin the pieces with their right sides together, beginning with the smallest (No. 4) triangles. Machine-stitch the pieces together, then stitch to a No. 3 pattern. Make another square like this. Join each to a No. 1 square to make the corner sections. Follow the diagram for colour positions.

TIPS

Accuracy in cutting and stitching is essential in patchwork of this type. Cut out carefully using sharp scissors.

Cotton fabrics are generally best. They do not fray or stretch easily and they press well.

When joining two pieces, pin at right angles to the seam. This enables you to machine-stitch across the pins without having to tack first.

Open out the seams to prevent bulkiness. Press only very lightly during the early stages; press well from the wrong side when the patchwork is complete.

CUTTING OUT THE FABRIC

From ivory fabric cut:

- ◆ 2 cushion backs
- ◆ 4 of pattern No. 1
- ◆ 4 of pattern No. 2
- ◆ 8 of pattern No. 4

From red spotted fabric cut:

- ◆ 4 of pattern No. 1
- ◆ 4 of pattern No. 3
- ◆ 8 of pattern No. 4
- ◆ 4 strips 36cm × 4cm/14in × 1½in for bindings

From plain red fabric cut:

- ◆ 1 of No. 1

2 Stitch two corner sections to a No. 2 pattern as shown. Stitch the remaining No. 2 patterns to the centre square, No. 1. Stitch the three sections together to form the cushion front.

3 Press all seams from the wrong side.

4 Machine-stitch a narrow double hem across one long edge of both cushion backs. Pin to the wrong side of the cushion front, matching the raw edges and corners, and overlapping at the centre. Pin and machine-stitch the right side of one binding piece to the right side of one cushion edge. The stitching should be 1.5cm/½in in from the raw edge. The seam allowance should be trimmed to 5mm/¼in.

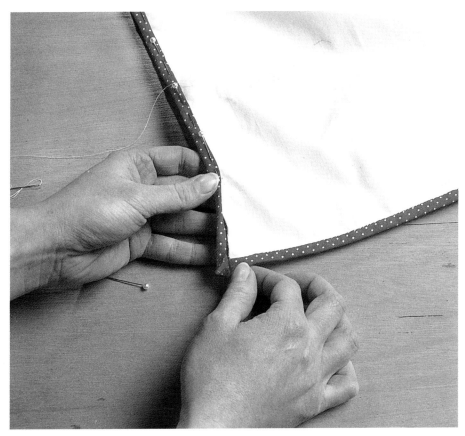

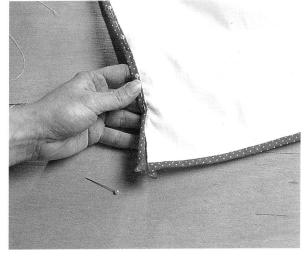

5 Turn the binding to the wrong side, then fold 5mm/⅜in along the raw edge, and pin in place. Slip-stitch the folded edge to the original stitching line. Bind the opposite side in the same way.

6 Apply bindings to the remaining two raw edges, tucking in the raw edges at all four corners. Stitch the corners neatly.

Appliqué Wall Hanging

Appliqué is an ancient art. Thousands of years ago, the Egyptians decorated their funeral tents with appliquéd work, and there are examples extant dating as far back as the 19th century BC. The art was brought to Europe during the Crusades, and used to apply coats-of-arms to banners as a signal to rally troops in battle. Appliqué became an important skill in quilt-making in later centuries in England and America. The "Little School House" motif featured in this wall hanging was a popular design for patchwork quilts during the 19th century. It was usually made from red and white fabric. The geometric shape lends itself well to appliqué work such as this. The main appliqué stitching is done by machine, with the decorative embroidery added by hand.

MATERIALS AND EQUIPMENT

- 1.3m/1½yd of 112cm/44in wide ivory cotton fabric

- 12 squares (20cm × 20cm/8in × 8in) of different patterned red and white cotton fabrics

- 20cm/8in of 112cm/44in-wide red and white gingham fabric for bindings

- 1m/1yd Bondaweb (doubled-sided adhesive paper for fabric)

- tracing paper, pencil and scissors

- sewing needles and pins

- matching sewing threads

- red stranded embroidery thread

- 60cm/23½in-long piece of narrow wooden dowel

1 Trace out the Little School House motif. Copy the motif on to the paper side of the Bondaweb in reverse. Cut out a Bondaweb square leaving about 2cm/¾in all around the motif. Iron the glue side on to the wrong side of each coloured fabric square.

Little School House motif – cut 12

cut out unshaded areas

(zigzag-stitch along solid lines)

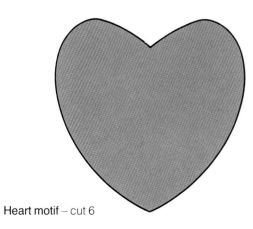

Heart motif – cut 6

THE ART OF THE NEEDLE

2 Cut out the house shape, then cut out the unshaded areas (refer to the template). Peel off the paper backings and position in the centre of the ivory squares. Press each one using a hot iron – the heat will melt the adhesive and fuse the two fabrics together.

3 Thread your sewing machine with red thread and using a 3mm-wide satin-stitch setting, sew over all the raw edges of the patterned motifs. Draw all the loose threads to the wrong side and finish off neatly.

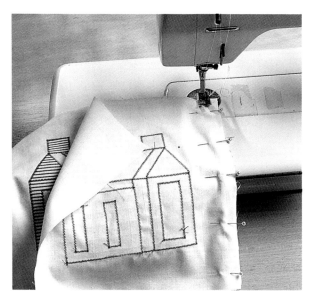

CUTTING OUT THE FABRIC

From ivory fabric cut:

◆ 1 piece 63cm × 83cm/25in × 33in for backing

◆ 12 23cm × 23cm/9in × 9in squares

From gingham fabric cut:

◆ 2 strips 4cm × 87cm/1½in × 34¼in and strips 4cm × 67cm/1½in × 26½in for bindings

◆ 4 rectangles 4cm × 6cm/1½in × 2⅜in for hanging loops

4 Machine-stitch the main squares, right sides together, to make a rectangle three squares across and four squares deep. Press all the seams open from the wrong side.

5 Using Bondaweb as before, cut out and iron on six small hearts at the points where the seams join. With three strands of red embroidery thread, blanket-stitch around the raw edge, and herringbone-stitch over all the seam lines.

6 Machine-stitch the right side of the longer binding pieces to the right side of the hanging, matching the raw edges. Turn the binding to the wrong side, then fold 1.5cm/⅝in along the raw edge. Pin and then slip-stitch the folded edge to the original stitching line.

7 Apply binding in the same way to the upper and lower edges. Tuck in the raw edges at all four corners, and stitch neatly.

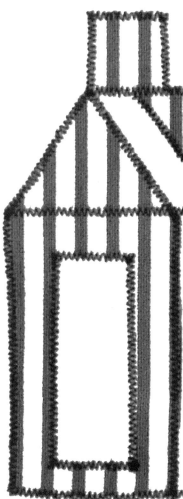

8 Machine-stitch a narrow hem on all four sides of the hanging loop pieces. Slip-stitch each piece to the wrong side of the hanging along the upper edge. Slot the wooden dowel through the loops and slip-stitch the open side at each end so that the dowel will not slip out. (The dowel can be removed when the hanging is cleaned.)

Cross-stitch Sampler

*Samplers used to be practice pieces for young needlewomen. They were
useful study aids – young girls learned their alphabet by embroidering
letters; they practised a whole vocabulary of stitches as they worked;
and they built up a repertoire of alphabets and motifs to use in future
needlework projects.*

*Today, samplers are worked purely for decorative purposes. This
sampler features the obligatory alphabet and numbers, a "Tree of Life"
motif, and brightly coloured parrots – not a standard motif in cross-
stitch, but a popular Pennsylvanian German motif in the 19th century.
Other popular motifs include pineapples (representing hospitality),
urns and flowers (symbolizing mourning), houses and trees.
Follow our colour scheme or be creative and design your own using
graph paper and coloured pencils. You can use the alphabet provided
to make your sampler more personal with a name or a
commemorative date.*

MATERIALS AND EQUIPMENT

- 50cm/20in square of 11-count embroidery canvas

- sewing needles, crewel needle, pins

- contrasting tacking thread

- stranded embroidery silk (refer to chart for colours)

- sharp embroidery scissors

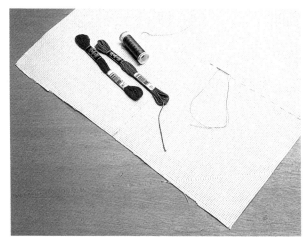

1 First locate and mark with tacking thread in a contrasting colour the centre of the canvas, both vertically and horizontally. This will give a reference point from which to begin the embroidery.

2 Cross-stitch is very simple to do. Using only three strands of embroidery thread at a time, work in horizontal rows from right to left.

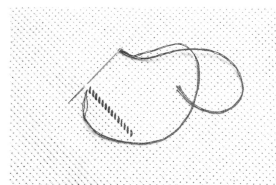

TIPS

Never cut more than 50cm/20in of thread at a time, to minimize tangling. Finish off the thread ends neatly on the wrong side as you go.
Count very carefully. Mistakes will throw the pattern out of line. Place marker pins every 10th thread. This will help when counting.

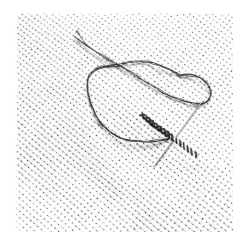

3 Return across the row from left to right, crossing each stitch.

4 Following the colour chart, begin at the centre, using the tacking threads as a guide. This will create a reference point from which to count to the other motifs. From the centre mark every 10th thread with a pin along the tacked lines. This will make the counting easier. Work the border small sections at a time. Continue following the chart until the sampler is complete.

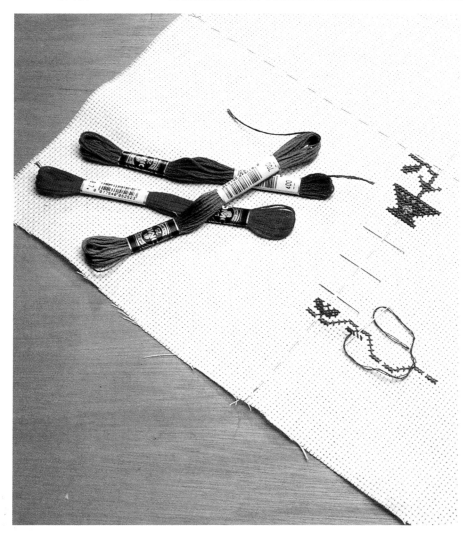

Amish-style Duvet Cover

*Amish quilts are noted for their bold colour combinations and simple
geometrical patterns – but if you look closely you see that large
expanses of colour are made up from many small squares.
Traditionally a layer of wadding would be sandwiched between the
patchwork layer and the backing piece, and then hand-quilted in
intricate patterns, which sometimes took many weeks or
months to complete.
This duvet cover is based on a traditional Amish design called
"Diamond In A Square", with the central square divided into a nine-
patch square. It is thought to have been inspired by the prayer books
the Amish brought with them to America, which had a central
diamond boss and a boss at each corner. This cover has all the visual
impact of a traditional quilt, but working it involves no hand-quilting.
It has a button opening through which you can insert your duvet.*

1 Begin by piecing small (No. 8) squares at the centre, then add on the surrounding border of Nos. 6 and 7 squares. Press each stage lightly, opening the seams where they join another edge. Follow the diagram below to complete the upper layer of the duvet cover.

Piecing arrangement

MATERIALS AND EQUIPMENT

- 1.7m/67in of 112cm/44in wide red cotton fabric

- 1.7m/67in of 112cm/44in wide green cotton fabric

- 2.2m/86½in of 112cm/44in wide blue cotton fabric

- 4.5m/180in of 228cm/89¾in wide red sheeting fabric (or two sheets)

- 8 red buttons

- matching sewing threads

- scissors

- sewing needles and pins

- plain pattern paper

- pencil

- ruler and set square

- tape measure

- tailor's chalk

DRAFTING THE PATTERNS

The diagram represents a scale pattern of a 200cm × 200cm/6½ft × 6½ft square. This will fit a double bed.
Use this diagram to piece together the cover. Trace on to plain paper the smaller pattern pieces, and mark the larger pieces with tailor's chalk on your fabric. Use a set square to check that all the right-angles are true.

PATTERN PIECE SIZES AND CUTTING INSTRUCTIONS

All pattern pieces include 1.5cm/⅝in seam allowance

Pattern 1: square 53cm × 53cm/21in × 21in cut 4 green

Pattern 2: rectangle 53cm × 103cm/21in × 40½in cut 4 blue

Pattern 3: square 15.5cm × 15.5cm/6in × 6in cut 4 green

Pattern 4: rectangle 15.5cm × 78cm/6in × 30¾in cut 4 red

Pattern 5: triangle with right-angle edges measuring 42.5cm/16¾in, cut 4 green

Pattern 6: square 9.25cm × 9.25cm/3⅝in × 3⅝in cut 4 blue

Pattern 7: rectangle 9.25cm × 40.5cm/3⅝in × 16in cut 4 red

Pattern 8: square 15.5cm × 15.5cm/6⅛in × 6⅛in cut 1 blue, 4 red, 4 green

Cut two large squares 203cm × 203cm/80in × 80in from the red sheeting fabric as a lining and a backing for the duvet.

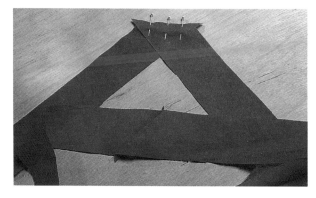

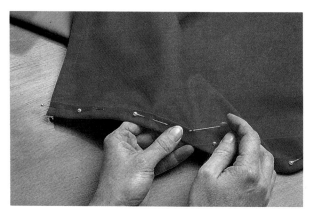

2 Cut approximately 11m/12yd of 7cm/2¾in-wide bias strips from the remaining red fabric. Stitch the strips together at right angles to make a continuous bias strip.

3 Tack the lining piece to the wrong side of the upper layer. Pin and stitch the right side of the binding to one edge of the upper piece. Turn the binding to the wrong side, fold 1.5cm/⅝in along the raw edge of the binding, then pin and slip-stitch the folded edge to the original stitching line. Apply binding to one edge of the backing piece in the same way. Tack the upper layer to the backing piece around the three raw sides.

4 Work 8 buttonholes evenly spaced along the binding of the backing piece. Sew on buttons to correspond on the upper layer. Fasten the opening. Apply bindings to the sides, tuck in the raw edges at the two lower corners. Bind and neaten the upper edge in the same way.

Baby Quilt

If you are beginning patchwork, a baby quilt is a good project to start with – it is a handleable size and small enough to be completed quite quickly. This quilt is based on the square patterns from which patchwork was made up. In this example, six "Evening Star" patchwork squares are joined together and lightly hand-quilted. The "Evening Star" is one of a group of classic star patterns in quilting. This cosy baby quilt is an average cot size and it makes a light, warm covering – not thick or heavy. Its polyester wadding filling traps the air, keeping the baby warm. Light quilting keeps the wadding fluffy, maintaining the insulation – the more hand-quilting you do, the flatter the quilt will become.

Blue star on white

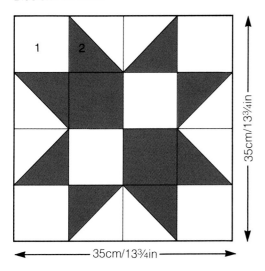

35cm/13¾in

35cm/13¾in

DRAFTING THE PATTERNS

Using the diagram (above) as a guide, draw a full-size pattern of one star square on to plain pattern paper. Cut out pattern pieces 1 and 2. Redraw these pieces adding a 1.5cm/⅝in seam allowance to all edges. The quilt is made up of six star squares, three blue stars on white, and three white stars on blue. Follow the larger diagram (right) as a guide to piecing.
Trace the heart-shaped quilting guide.

CUTTING OUT THE FABRIC PIECES

Pattern No. 1 – cut 24 white and 24 blue

Pattern No. 2 – cut 48 white and 48 blue

Cut one 73cm × 108cm/28¾in × 42½in rectangle of white for backing

Cut one 73cm × 108cm/28¾in × 42½in rectangle of wadding

Cut two 13cm × 85cm/5⅛in × 33½in strips and two 13cm × 120cm/5in × 47¼in strips from ticking for bindings.

105cm/41¼in

70cm/27½in

Note: reverse colours for white star on blue

MATERIALS AND EQUIPMENT

◆ 1.5m/60in of 112cm/44in-wide blue checked fabric

◆ 2.4m/96in of 112cm/44in-wide ivory cotton fabric

◆ 1.1m/43in of medium-weight polyester wadding

◆ 60cm/24in of 112cm/44in-wide blue and white cotton ticking for binding

◆ scissors

◆ sewing needles and pins

◆ matching sewing thread

◆ plain pattern paper

◆ pencil

1 Stitch together the centre four squares, then join the triangles together in pairs. Join the triangle squares together and stitch to the centre panel. Press all seams lightly, pressing them open. Make up three blue on white squares and three white on blue squares. Join them together using the large diagram opposite as a guide. Press all seams well from the wrong side.

2 Sandwich the wadding between the patchwork layer and the backing fabric. Pin at regular intervals all over the quilt.

3 Using a tacking thread in a contrasting colour, baste the three layers together. This will prevent slippage during hand-quilting.

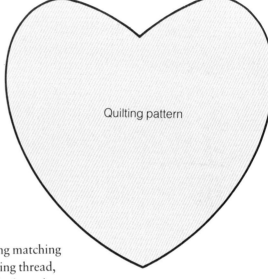

Quilting pattern

4 Using matching sewing thread, hand-quilt along the seam lines between each large square and around the centre square panels of each. The quilting stitch is a small running stitch taken through all three layers.

TIP

When hand-quilting, it is better to concentrate on making the stitches even rather than small.

---

5 Pin the heartshaped paper pattern to the plain white squares on the centre panel. Hand-quilt around the paper pattern.

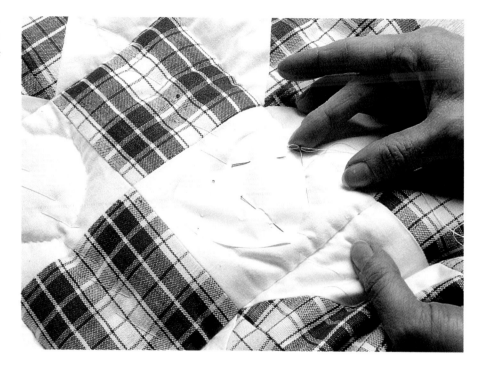

6 Stitch the right side of the shorter of the two binding strips to the right side of the quilt, matching the raw edges. Turn the binding to the wrong side and fold 1.5cm/⅝in along the raw edge of the binding. Pin and slip-stitch the fold to the original stitching line. Apply binding to the other two sides in the same way. Tuck in the raw edges at the four corners and slip-stitch neatly. This will make quite a wide edging.

TIME FOR TOYS

Rag Doll

Rag dolls are an old tradition. Their origins are now lost in time and much of their history is unrecorded, but they were probably originally made in poor homes from scraps saved from old clothes to be made into quilts, rugs and toys. Children still love their rag dolls.
Their attraction is that they are soft and cuddly – and, above all, individual. Every doll is different and has its own character sewn and embroidered into it.
Our rag doll is dressed in cotton poplin and gingham edged with broderie anglaise, with ribbon in her hair – but you can use any fabric scraps. The secret of a good doll is in the imaginative use of fabric, notions and embroidery to give her face a personality.

MATERIALS AND EQUIPMENT

◆ 40cm/16in of 112cm/44in-wide ivory cotton fabric

◆ 50cm/20in of 112cm/44in-wide blue gingham fabric

◆ 20cm/8in blue gingham fabric in a pattern of tiny squares

◆ 25cm/10in of 112cm/44in-wide white cotton poplin

◆ 1m/40in of white narrow broderie anglaise edging

◆ two squares of navy felt

◆ 8 small blue buttons

◆ 1m/40in narrow blue satin ribbon

◆ 100g/3½oz ball chunky knitting yarn for hair

◆ red stranded embroidery thread and scraps of felt for face

◆ 1m/40in red ribbon for hair bows

◆ scissors

◆ sewing needles and pins

◆ plain pattern paper, pencil and ruler

◆ fabric glue

◆ matching sewing threads

◆ bag of polyester toy filling

DRAFTING THE PATTERNS

Draft full-scale pattern piece using the pattern graph. Follow the cutting instructions and information written on the pattern pieces. Unless otherwise stated all seam allowances are 1.5cm/⅝in and are included in the pattern.

TIME FOR TOYS

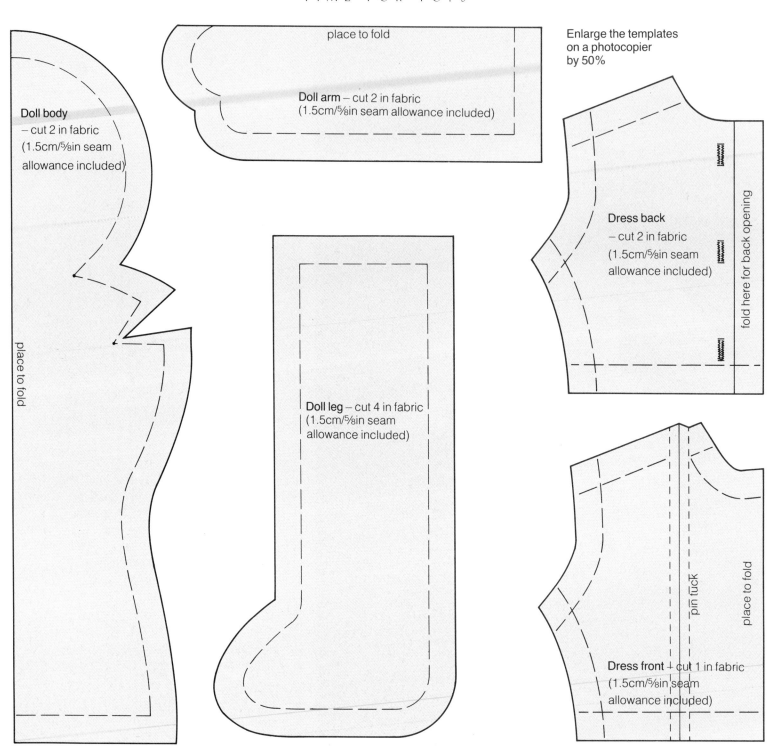

place to fold

Doll arm – cut 2 in fabric
(1.5cm/⅝in seam allowance included)

Enlarge the templates
on a photocopier
by 50%

Doll body
– cut 2 in fabric
(1.5cm/⅝in seam
allowance included)

Dress back
– cut 2 in fabric
(1.5cm/⅝in seam
allowance included)

place to fold

fold here for back opening

Doll leg – cut 4 in fabric
(1.5cm/⅝in seam
allowance included)

pin tuck

place to fold

Dress front – cut 1 in fabric
(1.5cm/⅝in seam
allowance included)

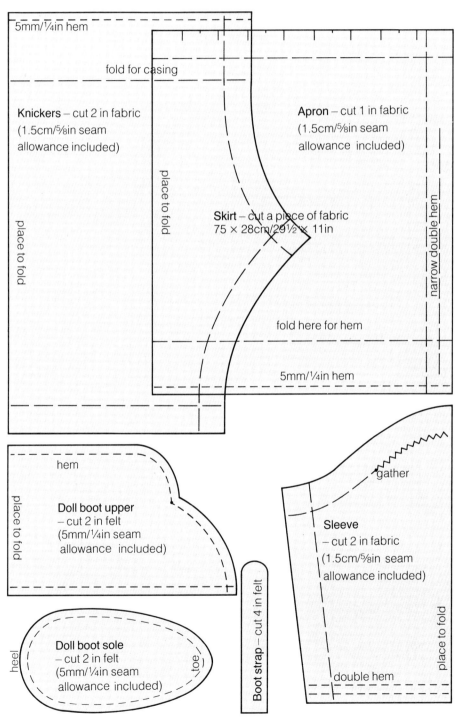

5mm/¼in hem

fold for casing

Knickers – cut 2 in fabric
(1.5cm/⅝in seam
allowance included)

place to fold

place to fold

Apron – cut 1 in fabric
(1.5cm/⅝in seam
allowance included)

narrow double hem

Skirt – cut a piece of fabric
75 × 28cm/29½ × 11in

fold here for hem

5mm/¼in hem

hem

place to fold

Doll boot upper
– cut 2 in felt
(5mm/¼in seam
allowance included)

heel

Doll boot sole
– cut 2 in felt
(5mm/¼in seam
allowance included)

toe

Boot strap – cut 4 in felt

gather

Sleeve
– cut 2 in fabric
(1.5cm/⅝in seam
allowance included)

place to fold

double hem

1 Machine-stitch the body and limb pieces right sides together as illustrated, leaving open the upper edges of the arm and leg join, and the lower edges of the body and arm join. Trim all seam allowances down to 5mm/¼in and snip into curved seams and to the small dot at the neck.

TIP

Use your imagination to create an individual expression for your doll. Embroider a mouth and glue on two small circles for the eyes.

2 Turn the arms through to the right side and stuff with toy filling. Tack across the upper edge, matching the seams. Tuck the stuffed arm inside the body and tack the arm into the arm join opening, matching the seams at the shoulder and side to the arm seam. Machine-stitch. Attach the other arm in the same way.

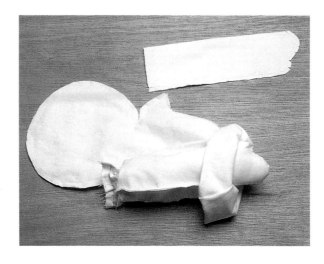

3 Turn the body to the right side. Turn the legs to the right side and stuff with toy filling. Tack across the upper edge, matching the seams. Tack the legs to one side of the lower edge of the doll body. Stuff the doll body with toy filling and then slip-stitch the lower body opening.

4 Cut out two knicker pieces as indicated. Stitch broderie anglaise to the lower edge of each leg. Press the seam to the wrong side and top-stitch. Machine-stitch the crotch seam together, then stitch the inside leg seam. Press 5mm/¼in, then 2.5cm/1in to the wrong side along the casing edge. Thread the casing with a 20cm/8in piece of narrow elastic, using a small safety pin. When it is threaded through, stitch the ends of the elastic together securely. Stitch a ribbon bow on each leg and on the front of the casing.

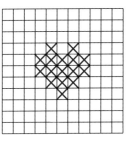

5 **Making the doll's dress** Machine-stitch the tuck down the centre front, then fold the centre back edge and work the buttonholes where indicated. Stitch the shoulder seams together. Stitch a narrow double hem at the wrist edge of both sleeves, then gather up the sleeve head between the small dots to fit into the armhole. Stitch the sleeves into the armholes, then join the side and sleeve seam in one. Cut a 75cm × 28cm/ 29½in × 11in band for the skirt, stitch the short edges together halfway up the seam. Fold and stitch a hem along the lower edge. Gather up the skirt to fit the waist, and machine-stitch in place. Stitch on the buttons to correspond with the buttonholes.

Making the apron Fold and stitch hems where indicated on pattern. Work cross-stitch motifs along lower edge following chart provided. Tack pleats at waist edge then stitch on the waistband/tie piece.

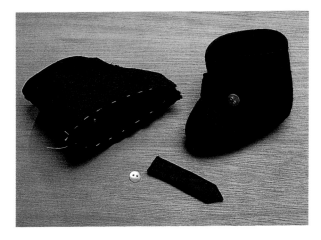

6 **The boots** Cut the boot pieces from the felt as indicated. Fold the boot upper in half at the centre back and stitch the front seam to the small dot. Fold and stitch a 5mm/¼in hem along the remainder of the upper edge. Stitch the sole to the upper, positioning the rounded end at the centre back. Turn the boots to the right side. Stitch the straps together in pairs very close to the edges. Stitch one end to the boot and fix the other end with a small button.

7 **The hair** Wind the knitting yarn into hanks about 40cm/16in long. You will need about six hanks for the hair. Wind a length of yarn around your thumb and little finger, as shown for the fringe.

8 Stitch the centre of the small hank to the forehead for the fringe, then stitch the centres of the other hanks down the back of the head. Tie the yarn in bunches at either side of the head.

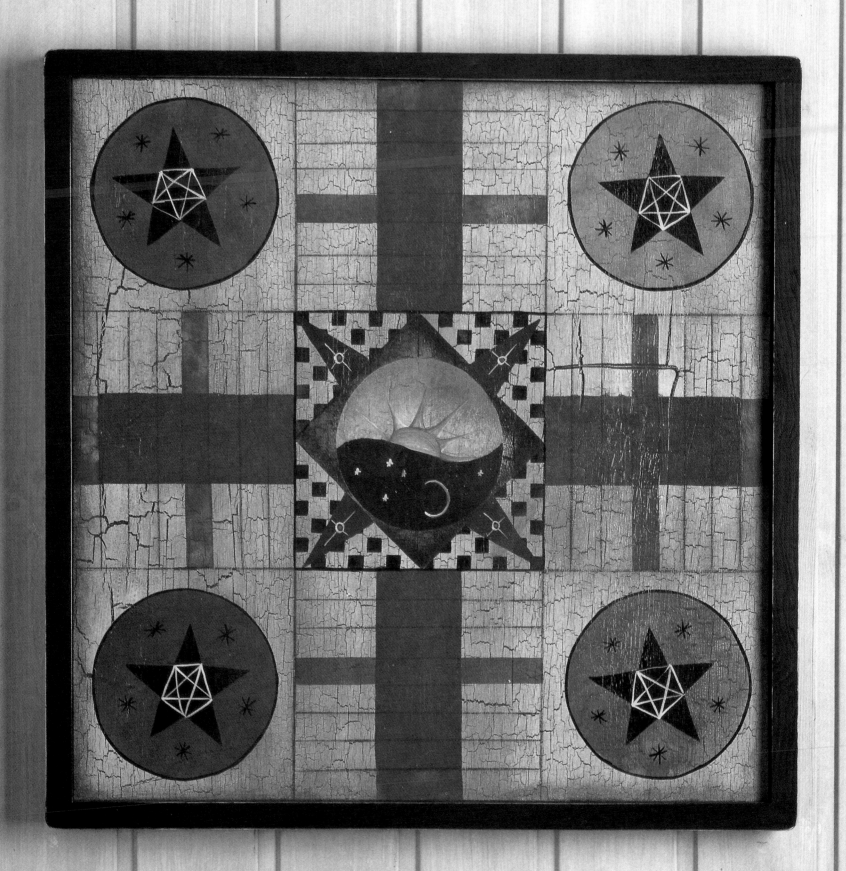

Game Boards

Folk art has a fine history of colourful painted boards for games like chess, draughts (checkers), and noughts and crosses (tic-tac-toe). During the 19th century the decoration of the boards became an art form – many were hung on the walls as decoration when not in use. The boards that are the theme of the next two projects are inspired by game boards made by amateur painters and sign painters for families on the North American frontier. The boards are easily made from plywood and painted with colourful emulsion paints.

The draughtboard on the following page has a decorated border – for players to put pieces on when not in play – with a central heart motif and colourful peacocks on either side. The secret of making a game board that looks authentic is to try to use the colours available to painters in the 19th century. Border designs should be painted in shades that mimic the earth pigments used at the time – brick reds, browns and ochres relieved by olive greens and mellow greeny blues.

The squares should be in darkest brown against parchment or buttermilk shades. Our board for noughts and crosses which follows, has counters made from squares of plywood sanded into smooth shapes. Afterwards you can make a drawstring bag to keep the board and counters together.

Draughtboard

MATERIALS AND EQUIPMENT

- 32cm × 52cm/12½in × 20½in piece of plywood
- wooden battens approximately 3cm/1¼in wide
- pencil
- ruler
- matt black emulsion paint
- cream emulsion paint
- acrylic paints, red, green, blue, black and white
- acetate film (for the stencil)
- tracing paper
- scalpel
- small paintbrushes
- 2.5cm/1in paintbrush
- small stencil brush
- tack hammer
- small hacksaw
- veneer pins
- wood glue
- sandpaper
- masking tape

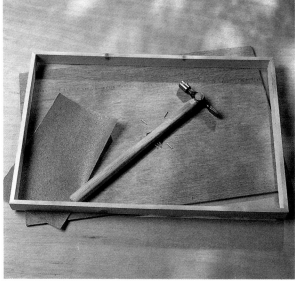

1 Cut the wooden battens into two 32cm/12½in and two 52cm/20½in lengths. Mitre the corners (cut them so that they make a 45° angle) carefully. Glue the frame together, checking the corners with a set square as you do so to make sure that the corners are perfectly square. When the glue is dry, hold the parts of the frame permanently together with veneer pins.

2 Glue and pin the frame to the base. Paint the frame and underside with matt black emulsion paint, and the face of the board with cream emulsion paint. Mark the checkerboard grid carefully with a pencil and ruler. Each square must be 3.5cm × 3.5cm/ 1⅝in × 1⅝in and the grid must have eight squares along each side. Paint the squares with black acrylic paint using a small brush. Rub away pencil marks with a soft eraser when the paint is completely dry.

Enlarge the stencil template on a photocopier by 25%

3 Trace and enlarge the stencil pattern. Cut a piece of acetate about 2cm/¾in larger all round than the pattern. Tape the acetate to the tracing and, using a scalpel, carefully cut out the design.

TIP

Acrylic paint are very quick-drying and so are ideal for stencilling. Practice stencilling on a spare sheet of paper before starting to decorate the board. It may take a few trial runs to get the colours and technique right.

4 Tape the stencil to the checkerboard. Mix the colours you require in a palette, to quite a thick consistency. Apply the paint sparingly with a stencil brush and a dabbing motion. Apply one colour at a time and mask off any areas you want to leave unpainted with masking tape. Allow each colour to dry before applying the next. Peel off the stencil and repeat the process on the other end of the board.

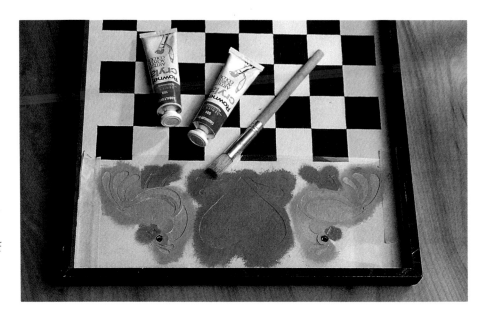

5 Paint in finer details with a small brush, using the picture opposite as a guide.

Noughts and Crosses

MATERIALS AND EQUIPMENT

- 12cm × 12cm/5in × 5in piece of plywood
- 2cm/½in wide wooden edging for frame
- 3cm/1¼in wide wooden batten for counters
- wood glue
- veneer pins
- tack hammer
- small hacksaw
- sandpaper
- matt black emulsion paint
- cream emulsion paint
- small paintbrush
- 1.5cm/½in paintbrush

TIP

To sand the counters: lay the sandpaper on your work surface and drag the edge of the counter along it until the corner is rounded.

1 Cut the wooden edging into four 11.5cm/4½in pieces. Butt the pieces together to fit the base. Glue and pin the frame.

2 Glue and pin the frame to the square base. Paint the frame and underside with matt black emulsion paint, and the face of the board with cream.

TIME FOR TOYS

3 Cut nine square pieces from the 3cm/ 1¼in-wide wooden batten, then sand the edges to smooth curves.

4 Paint each counter with matt black emulsion paint, then paint 0s on one side and Xs on the other with white acrylic paint.

WELCOME HOME

Candles

Herb Pot Stand and Sachets

Festive Garlands

Painted Chest

Candles

*Candlelight has a soft, golden glow that spreads an atmosphere of
serenity across a table or around a room. The mustardy-buff shade of
beeswax enhances the warmth of the light from candles made from
natural wax — candle-makers add some beeswax to paraffin wax to
give composition candles a natural colour.*

*You can make your own candles very simply from hand-rolled sheets
of the beeswax used by apiarists to line the hives as a base for the bees
to build their honeycombs. You can cut the sheets into strips to make
straight-sided candles, or triangles which, when rolled, make elegant
tapered candles. The beeswax sheets are imprinted with a hexagonal
honeycomb pattern which gives the finished candles a decorative
surface texture. When lit, the beeswax burns with a lovely fragrance.*

1 **Tapered candles** Cut the beeswax sheet in half diagonally using a scalpel and a metal ruler.

2 Cut a length of wick 2cm/¾in longer than the candle. Roll the edge of the beeswax sheet around the wick quite tightly, so that the wick is held firmly in place, then roll toward the tapered end, keeping the lower straight edge level. The beeswax sticks to itself.

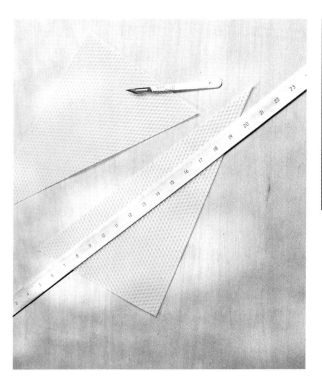

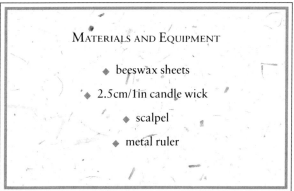

MATERIALS AND EQUIPMENT

◆ beeswax sheets

◆ 2.5cm/1in candle wick

◆ scalpel

◆ metal ruler

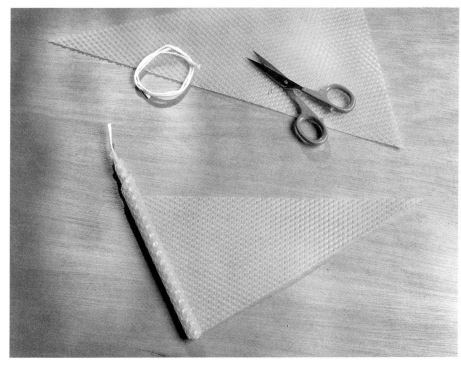

3 **Straight-sided candles** For straight-sided candles cut the sheet into straight strips.

Herb Pot Stand and Sachets

In the past herbs had many practical uses around the house. The scent of lavender and other herbs kept insects away, so they would be sprinkled on floors and under rugs, and hung from the rafters as an insect-repellent as well as an air freshener. "Washing herbs" would be added to the water in which bedlinen was washed to discourage bugs, and lavender was sewn into sachets, which would be placed among the folds of clothes stored in drawers and chests as moth-proofing.

The sachets were made from scraps of muslin and other loose-woven fabrics that would let the scent of the herbs seep through.

Dry your own herbs and flowers to make fragrant and colourful decorations for your home – bunches of herbs tied with fabric bows for the kitchen, and lavender sachets for the wardrobe. Or fill a pretty fabric pouch with bay leaves and cloves to use as a pot stand – the warmth of the room will release the scent of the herbs inside.

MATERIALS AND EQUIPMENT

◆ selection of fresh herbs and flowers (sage, bay, marjoram, lavender)

◆ cloves

◆ two 25cm/10in squares of lightweight, loosely woven fabric for the pot stand

◆ assorted ribbons and fabric strips

◆ thick cotton embroidery thread for tie-quilting

◆ sewing needles and pins

◆ scissors, bodkin and pencil

TIP

To make lavender hearts: stitch two fabric heart shapes right sides together, leaving a small gap in the stitching. Turn to the right side. Fill with lavender. Slip-stitch over the gap. Stitch on a ribbon bow and a hanging loop.

---

1 **Drying herbs and flowers** Preheat your oven to about 60°C (150°F). Tie the herbs or flowers loosely in small bunches, then arrange on a baking sheet with a space between each bunch. Place in the oven for about 45 minutes. Remove from the oven and allow to cool. Tie the bunches with pretty ribbons or fabric strips, or snip off the stems and remove the leaves with your hands for pot stands, sachets and other uses.

Alternatively you can tie the fresh herbs or flowers in bundles and hang them upside-down in a warm place to let them dry naturally. This may take several days.

2 **Pot stand** Stitch the two 25cm/10in squares together leaving a 4cm/1½in gap in the stitching on one side. Trim diagonally across each corner.

3 Turn the bag right side out and fill with dried bay leaves, herbs and cloves. Slip-stitch over the gap.

4 Using a bodkin and a double length of cotton embroidery thread pass the needle from the front through to the back and then to the front again. Tie the threads securely in a double knot, snip off the ends.

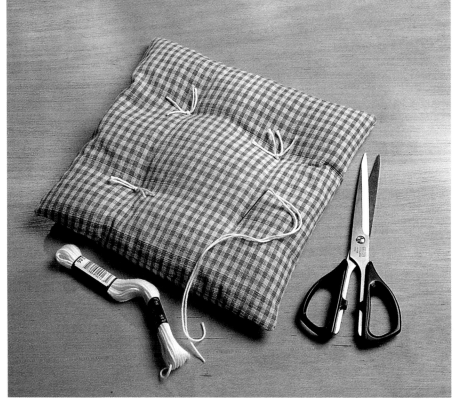

Festive Garlands

*Garlands turn an occasion into a festival and they are the perfect
ornament for seasonal festivities, from Easter to Christmas. There are
countless ways to adapt a basic garland design to make it appropriate
for any seasonal event. An Advent ring decorated with dried flowers is
easily converted into a spring garland with ivies and clematis.
Our unusual vine garland is designed for a harvest festival or an
outdoor party in autumn. It is entwined with vine leaves, hung with
black and white grapes, and finished with roses. In France's
Champagne region, many vine-growers plant bright red roses at the
ends of the rows of vines. The blooms help the growers make a simple
red-green colour vision test for an early warning of vine disease – if the
vines are sickly, the different shade of green will be immediately
apparent in contrast to the red of the roses. Our vine garland would
look pretty hanging on a door or a gate post, fixed to an outside wall –
or perhaps a vine plant – or laid on a garden table.*

1 Choose long, supple stems of vines or other climbing plants, such as clematis, that can be entwined around the ring. The stems must be in full leaf.

MATERIALS AND EQUIPMENT

◆ twisted twig-ring; ours was 30cm/11¾in in diameter

◆ stub wires

◆ wire cutters

◆ flower scissors or secateurs

◆ trails of vine leaves

◆ bunches of black and white grapes

◆ roses

2 Cut a stub wire in half and bend it to make a U-shaped staple. Place a stem over the ring and, where possible, push the stem end under the twig-ring binding. Fix the trailing stem to the twig-ring with a wire staple. Continue fixing stems to the ring until it is covered with stems and leaves.

3 Cut the grapes into small but dense bunches that will make the ring look abundant. Position the grapes over the ring so they will hang downward in a natural-looking way. Fix them to the ring by hooking a stub wire staple over the stem and into the ring.

TIP

Put the roses next to the black grapes, which will bring out their colour.

4 Attach the roses to one side of the ring (at about 11 o'clock) by threading the stems under the twig-ring binding.

Painted Chest

The samplers and quilts young girls used to make each year were stored in dower chests, ready for use when, as young women, they married. Solidly made of carved and decorated wood, the dower chest would be as large and impressive as the family could afford – the wealthier the family, the bigger and more magnificent the chest. Traditionally, dower chests were decorated with panels painted with the names of the owner and her family, and symbolic images such as unicorns, considered guardians of virginity. Later the husband's name would be added.

This project is a traditional dower chest design that you can use to decorate a wooden chest of any size. Our design was inspired by the "Star and Heart" appliqué motifs on a quilt made in 1875.

WELCOME HOME

1 First sand the chest to remove any old paint or varnish and to key the surface ready for painting. Wipe away dust with a soft cloth soaked in white spirit. Apply two coats of blue emulsion paint. Allow to dry. Trace the central motif and corner stars from the templates on page 106. You may need to extend the joining motif to fit the space on your chest. Tape the traced motifs to

squares of chalk-backed carbon paper of the same size.

2 Tape the paper patterns to the chest, positioning them carefully. Transfer the designs to the painted surface by tracing through the layers with a pencil.

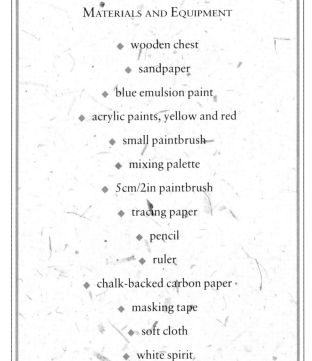

MATERIALS AND EQUIPMENT

◆ wooden chest

◆ sandpaper

◆ blue emulsion paint

◆ acrylic paints, yellow and red

◆ small paintbrush

◆ mixing palette

◆ 5cm/2in paintbrush

◆ tracing paper

◆ pencil

◆ ruler

◆ chalk-backed carbon paper

◆ masking tape

◆ soft cloth

◆ white spirit

WELCOME HOME

Joining motif
(extend to correct size)

corner motif – edge

main motif

3 Using a small paintbrush and red acrylic paint, carefully fill in the red areas of the design.

4 Allow the first painted sections to dry, then fill in the yellow areas. When the paint is dry, wipe the surface with a soft cloth soaked in white spirit to remove any remaining chalk marks.

CELEBRATIONS

Christmas Decorations

In Britain, as in most countries of northern Europe, evergreen branches and berries of holly, ivy, bay and mistletoe have for centuries been used to decorate houses at Christmas in addition to the appealing sight of festive foods and lights. The Christmas tree itself was brought to England from Germany in the 19th century by Prince Albert. Queen Victoria's husband.

Nowadays an enormous and elaborate selection of glass, metal, tinsel and wooden decorations can be bought, but there is no need to buy expensive Christmas tree decorations. Ornaments you make yourself are always much more original and satisfying. Here are some ideas for decorations to make for Christmas and other celebrations, from colourful scraps of fabric and ribbon, natural raffia, even brown paper, and pieces of shiny tin.

MATERIALS AND EQUIPMENT

- old tin cans (remove the lid and base and open the side piece)
  - tin snips
  - centre punch, tack hammer
  - fabric scraps
  - brown paper
  - natural raffia
  - ribbons
- thick cotton embroidery thread
  - bodkin
  - sewing needle and pins
  - scissors
  - tracing paper
  - pencil
  - hole punch
  - pinking shears
  - toy filling
- double-sided tape
  - masking tape

1 **Tin decorations**
Trace the pattern. Cut the basic shape from the tin with tin snips.

2 Tape the paper tracing to the tin shape. Punch along the pattern lines using the centre punch and a tack hammer. Tie on a ribbon hanging loop.

TIP

Use protective gloves when cutting the tin.

3 **Paper decorations**
Trace the pattern.
Cut out shapes from
brown paper with pinking
shears. Punch a row of
small holes around each
one, about 1cm/³⁄₈in in
from the edge, using a
hole punch.

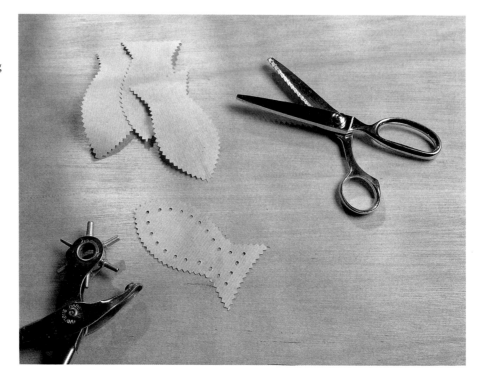

4 Stitch around the
edge using thick
embroidery thread and a
bodkin. Stick on a raffia
bow and a hanging loop
with double-sided tape.

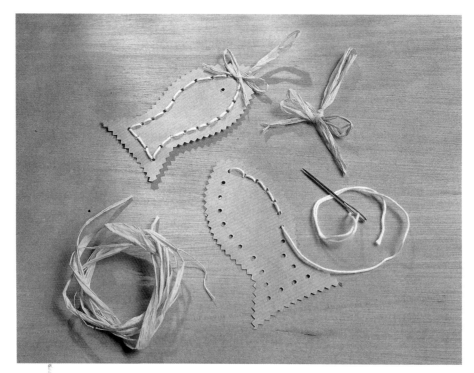

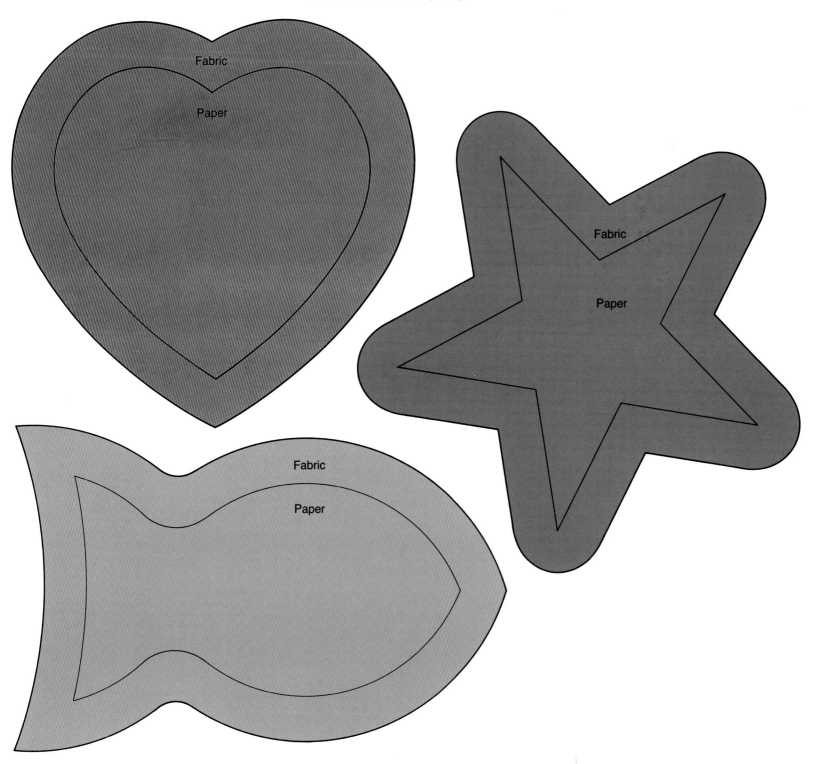

Fabric

Paper

Fabric

Paper

Fabric

Paper

CELEBRATIONS

5 **Fabric decorations**
Trace the pattern.
Cut two fabric pieces.
Machine- or hand-stitch
the pieces, right sides
together, 1.5cm/⅝in from
the raw edge. Leave a
3cm/1¼in gap in the
stitching on one side. Trim
the seam allowance to
5mm/¼in.

6 Turn the shape to
the right side and
press. Machine-stitch
about 5mm/¼in from the
edge, leaving the 3cm/
1¼in gap free. Stuff
lightly with toy filling.
Stitch over the gap and
stitch on a ribbon bow
and a hanging loop.

Heart and Hand Greeting Cards

*When paper, colourings, and pretty fabrics like satin and lace were
expensive and hard to come by, tokens of greeting were keepsakes to
be treasured for a lifetime. Even today, people appreciate the thought
and care that goes into designing and making a card for an important
occasion – a birthday, the birth of a child, an anniversary. A
beautifully made card is a keepsake, today as always. Our greetings
card of woven paper bears a symbolic heart and hand. A heart always
signifies love or romance, and it is believed that a hand-shaped card
harks back to an old English tradition of giving a glove to a lady as a
token of affection on St Valentine's day – because the word rhymes
with the word "love".*

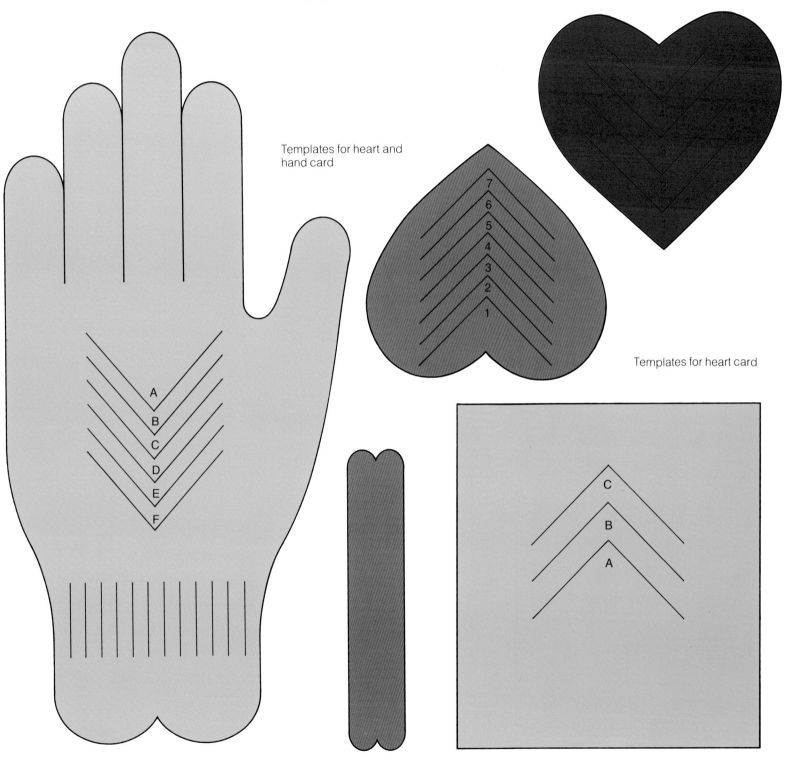

Templates for heart and hand card

Templates for heart card

1 Trace the template. Cut out the heart, hand and wristband with scissors. Make the diagonal cuts with a scalpel and a ruler.

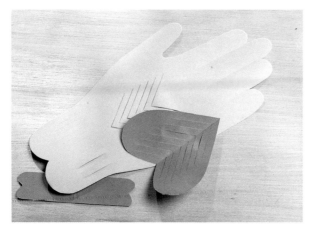

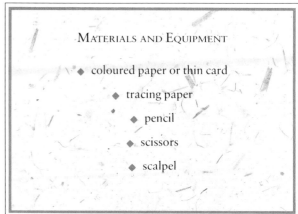

MATERIALS AND EQUIPMENT

♦ coloured paper or thin card
♦ tracing paper
♦ pencil
♦ scissors
♦ scalpel

2 Thread the band through the slots at the wrist. With the heart shape pointing toward the fingers, begin weaving the two pieces together. Tuck 2 under A, 3 under B, 4 under C, and so on. Push the heart shape up toward the fingers. Lift A and bring Point 3 up over the top. Weave 4 over B and tuck under A.

TIP

Mark the numbers and letters on the card lightly with pencil to avoid confusion.
Use the other templates to make smaller cards, the weaving method is the same.

3 Weave 5 over C, under B, then bring it out on top of A. Weave 6 over D, under C, over B, then tuck the point under A. Continue in this way to form the pattern.

4 Tuck all the numbered points in at the centre.

Cut Paper Projects

From China and Japan to the Middle East, Mexico and the Balkan countries cut paper designs have been a folk art for centuries. In eastern Europe peasants and farm workers hung paper-cutting "curtains" in the windows of their houses, and decorated the walls with cut-out paper patterns. Their intricate designs were made to keep, and appreciated as art, not throwaway decoration.

This heart-shaped cut out, surrounded by tulips is inspired by the delicate cut paperwork of a 19th-century Swiss woodcutter, Johan Hauswirth. Simple positive and negative effects are created by first folding a paper square into quarters, then cutting out a simple motif inspired by a design taken from an old Hawaiian appliqué quilt.

1 Fold a 22cm/8¾in square of paper into quarters, then trace the design of the folded paper motif on to it. Cut around the traced design with sharp scissors.

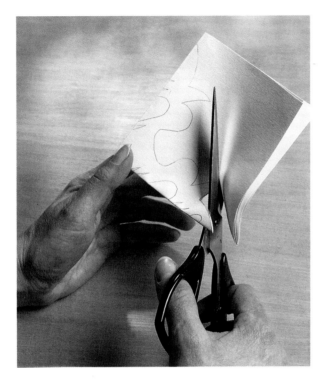

2 Open out the paper and glue it to a sheet of paper in a contrasting colour.

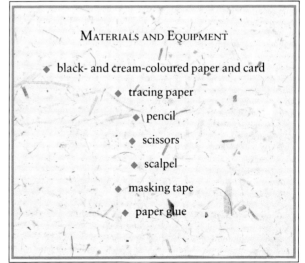

MATERIALS AND EQUIPMENT

- black- and cream-coloured paper and card
- tracing paper
- pencil
- scissors
- scalpel
- masking tape
- paper glue

3 Trace the design of the motif. Transfer it to black paper using chalk-backed carbon paper.

4 Cut away the main surplus areas with scissors, then work into the more detailed parts with a scalpel. Glue the finished cutout to a piece of card in a contrasting colour.

Cut paper motif

Folded paper motif

place to folded edge

place to folded edge

Fractur

The old art of Fractur practised by German settlers in North America has special relevance today, as the art of calligraphy is regaining popularity. A Fractur was a document – a record of some important anniversary or other event, written by a calligrapher who copied the details in a script similar to that used in medieval illuminated manuscripts (the German word Fractur *means "broken script"). Pennsylvanian settlers developed Fractur into a folk art form, decorating their commemorative scripts with drawings, motifs and mottoes. Hearts were often a central feature, surrounded by floral designs, and birds and animals were popular. Our design uses a traditional central heart bordered by tulips. You can substitute Gothic or italic script for the Fractur if you find it easier.*

1 Trace out the design, then transfer the design lines and calligraphy guide to the sheet of handmade paper. Now write the message. You may need to practise writing with the calligraphy pen on a spare sheet of paper.

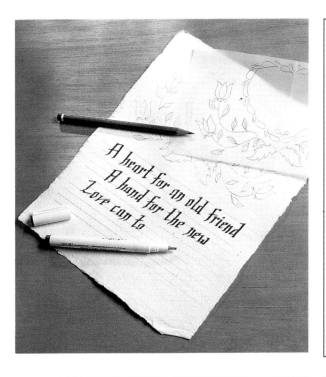

MATERIALS AND EQUIPMENT

◆ 20cm × 26cm/8in × 10¼in sheet of handmade paper

◆ acrylic paints, red, blue, green, yellow

◆ small paintbrushes

◆ tracing paper

◆ pencil

◆ ruler

◆ 2mm calligraphy pen

◆ coloured background paper

◆ picture frame

2 Paint in the coloured design using acrylic paints and a small paintbrush.

TIP

We used a small sheet of hand-made paper because it had a nice deckle edge. You could use a larger sheet of paper and tear the edge to create the same effect.

A heart for an old Friend
A hand for the new
Love can to earth lend
Heaven's hue

3 Mount the fractur on contrast coloured paper or fabric in a contrasting colour, then frame it. Write sayings, commemorative dates or greetings. This can make a really beautiful and personal gift for a special occasion.

INDEX